An Orange Tree Theatre production

POOR CLARE

by CHIARA ATIK

D1741963

ORANGE
TREE
THEATRE
A powerhouse of independent theatre

CAST

Francis **Freddy Carter**
Beatrice **Anushka Chakravarti**
Ortolana **Hermione Gulliford**
Peppa **Liz Kettle**
Beggar / The Poor **George Ormerod**
Clare **Arsema Thomas**
Alma **Jacoba Williams**

CREATIVES AND PRODUCTION TEAM

Writer **Chiara Atik**
Director **Blanche McIntyre**
Set and Costume Designer **Eleanor Bull**
Lighting Designer **Oliver Fenwick**
Sound Designer **George Dennis**
Casting Director **Annelie Powell CDG**
Voice and Accent Coach **Aundrea Fudge**

Assistant Director **Esther Fernández Guerra**
Costume Supervisor **Isobel Pellow**
Wigs and Hair Supervisor **Chris Smyth**
Design Mentee **Jennifer Wright**

Company Stage Manager **Jade Gooch**
Deputy Stage Manager **Jill Standish**
Assistant Stage Manager **Phoebe Butcher**
Stage Management Intern **Amelia Mehta**

Production & Technical Director **Phil Bell**
Production Technician **Andy Owen Cook**
Production Technician **Priya Virdee**

Special Thanks
Mountview Academy of Theatre Arts; London Academy of Music and
Dramatic Art; Dominique Hamilton; Emma Kylmälä; PJ McEvoy;
Holly Crewe; Jonathan Church Theatre Productions, with specific
thanks to Moé Saito.

Rehearsal photography © Ellie Kurttz

Chiara Atik Q&A

Playwright **Chiara Atik** sits down with the Orange Tree to discuss all things *Poor Clare*. Atik's *Poor Clare* received the 2022 American Theatre Critics Association's New Play Award, was the LA Drama Critics Circle winner for Best New Play, and a Susan Smith Blackburn Prize finalist. Her other plays include *Five Times in One Night*, *Bump*, and the comedy *Women*, a modern re-telling of *Little Women*. Discussing European debuts, contemporary writing, and intentions, Atik answers what we all want to know: Why *Poor Clare*?

Chiara, it's really exciting to have Poor Clare at the OT this Summer for its European debut. What about St Clare's story did you think was important to bring to the stage?

It is thrilling to have *Poor Clare* at the OT this summer! I started writing the play a few years ago, when I became uncomfortably aware of the gap between my empathy, and my ability – or rather willingness – to take action. In other words, I was doing a lot of hand wringing about the problems of the world – climate change, wealth inequality, political injustices – and not a lot of actually doing anything about it – certainly nothing that would compromise my own comfort.

Around this time, I remembered the story of Clare of Assisi, who, at 18, was able to do what I could never: walk away from her life, and dedicate herself to the betterment of others.

And so I started to write a play about Clare's radicalisation. What got her to that point? How was she able to do something that I know I never could? And if I can't go that far – how far could I actually go? And could that ever be 'enough'?

With the play set in Italy, and you being an American playwright, why do you think London is a great place to have its European debut?

The thing about cities is that the very rich and the very poor share the same public spaces. And if you share the same spaces, you are often confronted with people who have less money than you do. So how do we react to this? Does it make us uncomfortable? Do we train ourselves to ignore, to not notice? Do we feel bad every single time? Do we rationalize the disparity somehow?

This is a negotiation that I certainly experience in London as much as I do in New York, and in Los Angeles. So I think Londoners will be familiar with a lot of what's alluded to in the play, and hopefully some of the debate as well.

Humour is an integral part of *Poor Clare* as well as the modern form of speech. Is there a reason you decided to write this way?

Because I was writing the play in English, which is already so far removed from how 13th century characters in Assisi would have actually spoken, it felt more authentic to use contemporary vernacular and emotions. Had I tried to use some sort of faux-olde English as a swap for Umbrian, I worry the result would have been artificial, stilted, and – crucially – less funny. And humour is very important to me when I'm writing (or seeing!!) theatre. I'm happy to keep anachronisms if it makes the play funnier and the characters more relatable.

With themes of wealth distribution, religion, and politics being so prevalent in the show, audiences will surely see similarities to the world we're living in today. Was this something you thought about when writing the play?

Yes, very consciously. And there are moments in the play where the modern world purposefully and concretely pierces through the setting of the play, especially at the end.

And finally, if you had one wish with this play, whether that's what audiences take away from it, what the actors learn from being a part of it; what would it be?

I would love for the play to challenge us all – actors, audience, playwright! – to take a slightly less passive role as citizens of an unequal economic landscape. Of course, this will mean different things to different people. Donating more? Participating in direct aid, rather than just donating via third parties? Making eye contact with whomever is asking for spare change, even if you don't have any? Any additional awareness or consideration would be incredibly meaningful!

FREDDY CARTER
Francis

Theatre credits include: *The Wars of the Roses* (Rose Theatre Kingston); *Agnes Colander* (Theatre Royal Bath); *Lines in the Sand* (Soho Theatre); *All Day Permanent Red* (Royal Court Theatre) and *Circa* (The Vaults).

Television credits include: *Shadow & Bone*, *Masters of the Air*, *Maigret*, *The Doll Factory*, *Free Rein*, *15 Days* and *Pennyworth*.

Film credits include: *Wonder Woman*, *Heretiks* and *American Carnage*.

Voice credits include: *The Dagger and the Flame* and *Impact Winter*.

Freddy trained at The Oxford School of Drama.

ANUSHKA CHAKRAVARTI
Beatrice

Theatre credits include: *Coriolanus*, *The Crucible* (National Theatre); *Our Generation* (National Theatre and Chichester Festival Theatre); *The Divine Mrs S* (Hampstead Theatre) and *Girls Like That* (Birmingham Rep).

Television credits include: *Andor*, *Peacock* and *Jerk*.

Anushka studied at the University of Oxford before training at the Royal Central School of Speech and Drama.

HERMIONE GULLIFORD
Ortolana

Theatre credits include: *To Have and To Hold* (Hampstead Theatre); *The Southbury Child* (Bridge Theatre); *Romeo and Juliet* (Shakespeare's Globe); *3 Winters*, *Hotel* (National Theatre); *Love For Love*, *The Merchant of Venice*, *A Midsummer Night's Dream*, *Anthony and Cleopatra* (RSC); *The Way of the World*, *The Critic*, *The Real Inspector Hound*, *Three Sisters* (Chichester Festival Theatre); *Arcadia* (Bristol Old Vic); *The Country Wife* and *Twelfth Night* (Sheffield Crucible).

Television credits include: *The Chelsea Detective*, *Culprits*, *The Nevers*, *Doc Martin*, *Count Arthur Strong*, *Foyle's War*, *The Bletchley Circle*, *Call The Midwife* and *Upstairs Downstairs*.

Film credits include: *Cruella*, *Where Hands Touch*, *Stage Beauty* and *The Affair of the Necklace*.

Hermione trained at the Royal Central School of Speech and Drama.

LIZ KETTLE
Peppa

Theatre credits include:
Macbeth (An Undoing) (Rose Theatre, Kingston / Polonsky Shakespeare Theatre, New York / Royal Lyceum, Edinburgh); *Dracula – Mina's Reckoning* (National Theatre of Scotland); *Richard III* (Rose Theatre, Kingston / Liverpool Playhouse); *The Girl on the Sofa* (Royal Lyceum Theatre, Edinburgh / Berlin Schaubühne / Thomas Ostermeier); *Henry VI* (RSC); *The Tempest* (Tron Theatre, Glasgow); *Waves, The Seagull, Attempts On Her Life* (National Theatre / European Tour / Broadway); *Catch 22* (Northern Stage); *TRUTH – Song Theatre* (National Tour); *Richard III, Taming of the Shrew* (Shakespeare's Globe); *Iphigenia at Aulis* (Abbey Theatre, Dublin); *The Roaring Girl's Hamlet* (Sphinx Theatre Co.); *Plasticine* (Royal Court); and *The Tempest* (Schauspielhaus Köln / Hamburg).

Television credits include: *The Crown, Unforgotten IV, Paris with Alexei Sayle, The Secret Life of Mrs Beeton, Doctors, Jeeves & Wooster, Inspector Morse, Rosemary & Thyme* and *Poirot*.

Film credits include: *Fracture, Between Us* and *The Final Journey*.

Radio credits include: *Keli, Daughters of Brittania*.

GEORGE ORMEROD
Beggar / The Poor

Theatre credits include: *Henry V, The Complete Works of William Shakespeare* (The Attic Theatre) and *Othello* (Worcester Repertory Company).

George trained at the Royal Welsh College of Music & Drama.

ARSEMA THOMAS
Clare

Poor Clare is Arsema's stage debut.

Television credits include: *Queen Charlotte: A Bridgerton Story.*

Film credits include: *She Taught Love* and *Fall 2.*

Arsema trained at LAMDA and is a graduate of Yale University and Carnegie Mellon University.

JACOBA WILLIAMS
Alma

Theatre credits include: *Pinocchio* (Watermill Theatre); *Macbeth, Hamlet* (Shakespeare's Globe Prison Project); *The Frogs* (Kiln Theatre / Royal & Derngate); *Women & Theatre: Revival* (Birmingham Rep); *Twelfth Night For One Night Only, The Fir Tree, A Midsummer Night's Dream,*

Twelfth Night (Shakespeare's Globe); *The Winter's Tale, Our Verse in Time* (Sam Wanamaker Playhouse); *Where Do We Go From Here? (*Pentabus Theatre); *Alice in the Universe* (Oxford Playhouse); *Bogeyman* (Pleasance Dome); *Before I was a Bear* (Bunker Theatre / Soho Theatre); *Gulliver's Travels* (Unicorn Theatre); *Love Dance* (Chiswick Playhouse); *The Snow Queen* (Stephen Joseph Theatre, Scarborough); *When the Sea Swallows Us Whole* (Vaults Festival) and *Queens of Sheba* (Camden People's Theatre / New Diorama / Underbelly / Vaults Festival – Winner of The Stage Award 2018).

Television credits include: *Pushers*, *Vera* and *Twelfth Night*.

Short film credits include: *Framed*, *The Vest*, *Highlife*, *Montague*, *Cleo's Choice* and *Expiry Date*.

Radio credits include: *Bleak House*, *Vergil* and *Precious Little Thing*.

Jacoba trained at Italia Conti Academy of the Arts and the National Youth Theatre.

CHIARA ATIK
Writer

Chiara Atik is a playwright and screenwriter. Her play *Poor Clare* was the recipient of the 2022 American Theatre Critics Association's New Play Award, the LA Drama Critics Circle winner for Best New Play, and was a Susan Smith Blackburn Prize finalist.

Other plays include *Five Times in One Night*, *Bump*, and the comedy *Women*, a modern re-telling of Louisa May Alcott's *Little Women*, which was a New York Times Critic's Pick for Comedy and won the Hollywood Fringe Festival. Chiara is a member of the Ensemble Studio Theatre. She splits her time between New York and Los Angeles.

BLANCHE MCINTYRE
Director

Theatre credits include: *The Merry Wives of Windsor*, *All's Well That Ends Well*, *Titus Andronicus*, *The Two Noble Kinsmen* (RSC); *Antony and Cleopatra*, *Twelfth Night: For One Night Only*, *Measure for Measure*, *Bartholomew Fair*; *The Winter's Tale*, *As You Like It*, *The Comedy of Errors* (Shakespeare's Globe); *The House of Shades*, *Hymn*, *The Writer* (Almeida Theatre); *Letters from Max*, *Apex Predator*, *The Invention of Love*, *Botticelli in the Fire* (Hampstead Theatre); *Tartuffe* (National Theatre); *Arabian Nights*

(Bristol Old Vic); *The Norman Conquests* (Chichester Festival Theatre); *Noises Off* (Nottingham Playhouse); *Welcome Home, Captain Fox!* (Donmar Warehouse); *The Oresteia* (HOME, Manchester); *Super High Resolution* (Soho Theatre); *Arcadia* (ETT); *Women in Power*; *Tonight at 8:30*; *The Nutcracker* (Nuffield Southampton Theatres); *Ciphers* (Out of Joint / Bush Theatre / Exeter Northcott); *The Birthday Party* (Manchester Royal Exchange); *The Seagull* (Headlong / Nuffield Southampton Theatres / Derby Theatre); *The Seven Year Itch* (Salisbury Playhouse); *Accolade*, *Foxfinder* and *Molière or The League of Hypocrites* (Finborough Theatre).

Opera includes: *Tosca* and *The Marriage of Figaro* (ETO).

ELEANOR BULL
Designer

Eleanor is an award-winning Set and Costume Designer across theatre, dance, opera, and film. In 2017, she won the Linbury Prize for Stage Design and in 2020 she was nominated by Shakespeare's Globe for The Evening Standard Future Theatre Award.

Following her contribution as 'Costume Design Assistant and Concept Work' on Yorgos Lanthimos' *Poor Things*, Eleanor was honoured as part of the film's Costume Team, which won both an Academy Award and a BAFTA for Costume Design, under Costume Designer Holly Waddington.

Orange Tree Theatre design credits include: *That Face*, *The Tempest*, *Katie Johnstone* and *In the Night Time (Before the Sun Rises)*.

Other design credits include: *The Snowmaiden*, *Blond Eckbert* (English Touring Opera); *The Importance of Being Earnest* (Manchester Royal Exchange); *Suddenly Last Summer* (English Theatre Frankfurt); *Death Trap/ Cerberus* (Rambert / Ben Duke); *Wired to the Moon* (Ballet Cymru UK Tour); *Mushy: Lyrically Speaking* (Watford Palace Theatre / Rifco); *Tin Man, and PULSE!* (Joss Arnott Dance); *Glory* (Red Ladder UK Tour); *Stop and Search* (Arcola Theatre); *American Idiot* (Mountview); *Isaac Came Home from the Mountain* (Theatre503); *Windrush: Movement of the People* (Leeds Playhouse / UK Tour / BBC broadcast); *Julius Caesar* (Costume Design – Bristol Old Vic); *Crave* (The Wardrobe Theatre) and *The Two Gentlemen of Verona* (The Redgrave Theatre).

OLIVER FENWICK
Lighting Designer

Theatre credits include: *Alterations*, *Dear Octopus*, *The Father and the Assassin*, *Blues* for an Alabama Sky, Kerry Jackson, Tartuffe – the Imposter, The Great Wave, Ugly Lies the Bone and The Motherfucker with the Hat, Happy Now?, The Holy Rosenburgs (National Theatre); The School for Scandal, The Magician's Elephant, Love's Labour's Lost, Much Ado About Nothing, The Jew of Malta, Wendy and Peter Pan, The Winter's Tale, The Taming of the Shrew, Julius Caesar (RSC); Clyde's, Sweat, Trouble in Butetown, One Night in Miami, The Vote, Berenice (Donmar Warehouse); Ulster American (Riverside Studios); My City and Ruined (Almeida Theatre); Red Velvet (Kiln Theatre / St Ann's, New York); Handbagged (Kiln Theatre / West End); The Purists, The Invisible Hand, Holy Sh!t, White Teeth, Paper Dolls (Kiln Theatre); Murder on the Orient Express (UK Tour); The Cabinet Minister, Power of Sail, A Number, Travels with My Aunt (Menier Chocolate Factory); The Cord, The Arrival (Bush Theatre); Girls & Boys (Royal Court Theatre / New York); Lela & Co, Routes, The Witness, Disconnect (Royal Court Theatre); Hansel And Gretal, To Kill a Mockingbird, Hobson's Choice (Regent's Park Open Air Theatre); Saved, A Midsummer Night's Dream (Lyric Hammersmith); Reykjavik, Gloria, Occupational Hazards, Reasons to Be Happy, Private Lives, The Giant, Glass Eels, Comfort Me with Apples (Hampstead Theatre); Oleanna, King Lear, Di, Viv and Rose, The Importance of Being Earnest, Bakersfield Mist, Kean, The Madness of George III and Ghosts (West End).

GEORGE DENNIS
Sound Designer

Theatre includes: Alterations; Blues for an Alabama Sky; An Octoroon (National Theatre); Twelfth Night; Love's Labour's Lost; Venice Preserved (RSC); Keli (National Theatre Scotland); The Homecoming – Olivier Award nomination for Best Sound Design (Trafalgar Theatre); The Seagull; Lemons Lemons Lemons Lemons Lemons; Pinter at the Pinter 1, 2 & 7 (Harold Pinter); The Effect (The Shed, NY/National Theatre); English (Kiln Theatre / RSC); Roots; The Duchess of Malfi; Three Sisters (Almeida Theatre); The Cabinet Minister (Menier Chocolate Factory); The Homecoming; Further Than The Furthest Thing; The Mountaintop (Young Vic); Straight Line Crazy (The Shed, NY/Bridge Theatre); Nine Night (Trafalgar Theatre / National Theatre); The Importance of Being Earnest (Vaudeville); Mom, How Did You Meet The Beatles; Sing Yer Heart Out For The Lads; The Deep Blue Sea; The Norman Conquests (Chichester Festival Theatre); A Taste of Honey; Glee & Me (Royal Exchange); The Southbury Child; Two Ladies (Bridge); Talent; Frost/Nixon; Tribes (Crucible Theatre); Hedda Tesman; Spring

Awakening (Headlong); *Much Ado About Nothing*; *Imogen*; *The Taming of the Shrew* (Globe); *Harrogate*; *Fireworks*; *Liberian Girl* (Royal Court) and *Julie* (Internationaal Theater Amsterdam).

ANNELIE POWELL CDG
Casting Director

Annelie Powell CDG is a Casting Director for theatre, television and film. She is also currently a Creative Associate at Jonathan Church Theatre Productions.

Orange Tree Theatre credits include *Playhouse Creatures* directed by Michael Oakley (also UK tour).

Annelie works prolifically with a variety of theatres on a freelance basis with recent credits that include: *Wendy & Peter Pan* directed by Jonathan Munby (RSC / Barbican); *Treasure Island*, directed by Paul Foster (Bristol Old Vic Theatre); *The Enormous Crocodile* directed by Emily Lim (Regent's Park Open Air Theatre / UK Tour); *Apex Predator* directed by Blanche Mcintyre (Hampstead Theatre); *Kathy & Stella Solve A Murder!* directed by Jon Brittain and Fabian Aloise (West End); *Now That's What I Call A Musical!* directed by Craig Revel Horwood (UK Tour); *Wonder Boy* directed by Sally Cookson (Bristol Old Vic Theatre / UK Tour); *The Promise* directed by Jonathan Kent (Chichester Festival Theatre);

Coram Boy directed by Anna Ledwich (Chichester Festival Theatre); *Taste of Honey* directed by Emma Baggott (Manchester Royal Exchange); *In Dreams* directed by Luke Sheppard (Leeds Playhouse) and *House of Shades* directed by Blanche McIntyre (Almeida Theatre).

Annelie's television work includes projects with Netflix, Apple, Warner Brothers, Hallmark, BBC and ITV in addition to her work on Independent Feature Films and Adverts.

AUNDREA FUDGE
Voice and Accent Coach

Aundrea Fudge is an accent/dialect and speech coach from New York. She completed her MFA in Voice Studies from the Royal Central School of Speech and Drama in 2018 and is currently based in London where she currently teaches and runs accent workshops for Royal Central School of Speech and Drama, Royal Academy of Dramatic Arts, and Guildhall School of Music and Drama.

Orange Tree Theatre credits include: *In Praise of Love*, *Here in America*, *Red Speedo*, *Meetings* and *Yellowman*.

Other theatre credits includes: *Good Night Oscar* (Barbican); *Clueless* (Trafalgar Theatre); *The Crucible* (Shakespeare's Globe); *Slave Play* (Noël Coward Theatre); *Fear of 13*, *Skeleton Crew*,

Clyde's (Donmar Warehouse); The Beautiful Future is Coming, Reverberation, Choir Boy (Bristol Old Vic); The House Party (Chichester Festival Theatre); A Raisin in the Sun, A View From The Bridge (UK Tour / Headlong); Start Swimming! (Young Vic Theatre); Shucked, The Enormous Crocodile, Once on this Island (Regents Park Open Air Theatre); East is South, Between Riverside and Crazy, Blackout Songs (Hampstead Theatre); Wish You Were Here, Bootycandy (Gate Theatre); Refilwe (Bernie Grant Arts Centre); Cinderella (Brixton House); Driving Miss Daisy (Barn Theatre) and Bring it on! The Musical (Southbank Centre).

Film credits includes: Bernard & The Genie, Locked In-Film and Wheel of Time.

Television credits includes: The Buccaneers (Season 2) and Andor (Season 2).

ESTHER FERNÁNDEZ GUERRA
Assistant Director

Esther Fernández Guerra is a theatre director and writer from the Canary Islands. She started her artistic career as a dancer and has over 15 years of training as a ballet dancer. After that, Esther studied acting in Escuela de Actores de Canarias, where she learned a very physical approach to theatre and character construction.

This combination of drama and dance makes her a very versatile and creative artist, with a strong movement approach to theatre. Esther is currently studying an MA in Directing at LAMDA.

Directing credits include: Borderline (Lion and Unicorn Theatre).

Associate director credits include: Crazy Gary's Mobile Disco (Landor Space) and The White Plague (Greenwich Theatre).

Assistant director credits include: Alice (Landor Space) and Property (New River Studios).

ISOBEL PELLOW
Costume Supervisor

As Costume Supervisor: Retrograde (Apollo Theatre); 4.48 Psychosis, More Life (Royal Court Theatre); Princess Essex (Shakespeare's Globe); Kathy and Stella Solve A Murder (Ambassadors Theatre); Bronco Billy (Charing Cross Theatre); Jack and the Beanstalk (Theatre Royal Stratford East); The Ballad of Hattie and James, Mlima's Tale, Girl on an Altar (Kiln Theatre); The Walworth Farce (Southwark Playhouse); A Christmas Carole (Southend Palace); Alice in Wonderland (Brixton House); The Memory of Water, Blackout Songs (Hampstead Theatre); House of Flamenka (Peacock Theatre); Green Eggs and Ham (Opera North); The Sweet Science of Bruising, Britten in Brooklyn

(Wilton's Music Hall); *Four Play* and *Clickbait* (Theatre503).

As Costume Designer: *Twelfth Night* (Theatre on Kew); *Death Drop* (West End / UK Tour); *The Lay of the Land* (The Place); *Yes So I Said Yes*, *Not Quite Jerusalem*, *The Wind of Heaven* (Finborough Theatre); *Lysistrata* (The Cockpit); *Heather and Harry* (Camden People's Theatre); *King Lear* (Pleasure Dome Theatre Company); *'Tis Pity She's A Whore* (Tristan Bates Theatre) and *Tales of Offenbach* (Wilton's Music Hall).

Isobel trained at the London College of Fashion.

CHRIS SMYTH
Wigs and Hair Supervisor

Orange Tree Theatre credits include: *Churchill in Moscow*, *Treasure Island*, *Twelfth Night*, *Suite in Three Keys*, *Testmatch*, *Uncle Vanya*, *She Stoops To Conquer* and *The Circle*.

Theatre credits include: *The Forsyte Saga* (Park Theatre); *The Drifters Girl* (UK Tour); *The Circle* (UK Tour); *Guys and Dolls* (Bridge Theatre); *Pretty Woman* (Savoy Theatre) and *9 to 5* (UK Tour).

JILL STANDISH
Deputy Stage Manager

Jill is a stage manager with several decades of experience and specialises in the role of Deputy Stage Manager. She has worked on many different styles of productions including UK and International Touring Theatre, West End, Regional and Educational Theatre and across various genres including plays, musicals, opera, and ballet.

Theatre credits include: *To Have and To Hold* (Hull Truck Theatre); *These Majestic Creatures* (Stephen Joseph Theatre, Scarborough); *Brassed Off* (Durham Gala Theatre); *Awful Auntie* (UK Tour / International Tour); *40 Years of Phoenix* (UK Tour); *Les Miserables* (West End); *The Wedding Singer, Carrie the Musical* (Urdang); *Sleeping Beauty*, *Aladdin* (Lighthouse, Poole); *The Land of Might Have Been*, *Viva La Diva* (Buxton International Opera Festival); *La Cambiale di Matrimonio* (Royal Academy of Music) and *Snow White* and *Anne of Green Gables* (London Children's Ballet).

PHOEBE BUTCHER
Assistant Stage Manager

Phoebe is a London-Based Stage Manager, with focus on queer theatre and Book Cover/ DSM roles. Their previous work includes *Mouth of the Gods* (ASM – Border Crossings / Hoxton Hall); *Sherlock Holmes and the Poison Wood* (ASM – Watermill Theatre) and *Crying Shame* (SM on Book – Sweet Beef Theatre / Pleasance Dome).

This is their first show with

the Orange Tree, and they are very excited to work with this wonderful team.

AMELIA MEHTA
Stage Management Intern

Amelia Mehta is a second-year student studying Drama and Creative Writing at Royal Holloway, University of London, where she has developed a deep passion for playwriting alongside directing and stage production.

Being a member of her Musical Theatre Society and Drama Society, she has worked in backstage management, lighting and stage design, and technical operations. Amelia is looking forward to working on *Poor Clare* and gaining a lot of valuable experience at the OT.

ORANGE TREE THEATRE

A powerhouse of independent theatre

We are a local theatre with a global reputation.

A show at the Orange Tree is close-up magic: live, entertaining, unmissable. We're an intimate theatre with the audience wrapped around the stage. We believe in celebrating what it means to be human. We believe in putting people at the centre of the stories we tell. And we believe in the power of a writer's words, an actor's voice, and an audience's imagination to transport us to other worlds and other lives.

We punch above our weight to create world-class productions of new and contemporary drama, revitalise classics and re-discoveries, and introduce children and young people to the magic of theatre.

We are deeply rooted in our local community in South West London. We work with thousands of people aged 0 to 100 in Richmond and beyond through participatory theatre, bringing generations together to build confidence, connection, and joy. Our ground-breaking Primary Shakespeare and Shakespeare Up Close projects pack the theatre with children and ignite a spark to last a lifetime.

We're a registered charity (266128). With only 180 seats and no support from Arts Council England, we rely on the generosity of our audiences and donors to raise £650,000 a year. These funds support our outstanding work on stage and in the community and invest in the next generation of talent.

Artistic Director **Tom Littler**
Executive Director **Julie Weston**

orangetreetheatre.co.uk

LONDON BOROUGH OF
RICHMOND UPON THAMES

THEATRE OF THE YEAR

THE STAGE AWARDS

OT TEAM

Executive
*Artistic Director
& Joint CEO*
Tom Littler
*Executive Director
& Joint CEO*
Julie Weston
Executive Assistant
Reya Muller

**Producing &
Programming**
*General Manager
& Producer*
Sarah Murray
Carne Associate Director
Georgia Green**
Literary Associate
William Gregory
*Associate Casting
Director*
Annelie Powell *
*Trainee Production
Assistant*
Hetty Opayinka

**Production &
Technical**
*Production &
Technical Director*
Phil Bell
*Company Stage
Manager*
Jade Gooch
*Senior Production
Technician*
Andy Owen Cook
Production Technician
Priya Virdee

Development
Development Director
Dominique Trotter
Development Manager
Katie Devey
Development Officer
Rosa Stilitz

Community
Community Director
Francesca Ellis
Community Manager
Madi Mahoney
Community Associate
Jess Haygarth
Community Facilitators
**Jordana Golbourn
Amy Tickner**
Community Assistants
**Heavadny Dianne C
Sophie Kenyon
Ethan Simm**

Marketing & Sales
*Marketing & Sales
Director*
Thomas Atkinson-Joy
Marketing Officer
Hannah McLelland
*Box Office & Sales
Coordinator*
Addie Uglow
Box Office Assistant
Sophie Kenyon
Graphic Designer
Annie Rushton*
PR
Kate Morley PR*
Box Office Team
**Léonie Crawford
Madeleine Paine**

**Finance, HR &
Operations**
Finance Manager
Caroline Goodwin
Finance Associate
Jodie Cramphorn*
Finance Assistant
Nida Zamir
HR Consultants
**Bendy Ashfield,
Greg Jauncey for
Theatre People***

Customer Service
Front of House Manager
George Holmes
Duty Managers
**Léonie Crawford
Andrew Davidson
Tyler Deniro
Jay Hannaford
Madeleine Paine
Fenella Machin**
Stewards
**Ailsa Auchnie
Eden Igwe
Emeka Agada
Juliet Mills
Kaitlin Reynell
Kevin Mandry
Lucy Greenhalgh
Luiza McDowell
Maire McGovern
Martha Barnett
Penny Cranford
Shane Convery
Roanna McIvor
Irie Page
Daisy Shaw
Tomas Caldon**
*Cleaner (from Miss Merry
Cleaning Services)*
Viktor Kirov

Board Members
**Feras Al-Chalabi
Anita Arora
Carolyn Backhouse
Richard Buxton
Judy Gibbons** (Chair)
**Lesley Gregory
Marina Jones
Victoria Kent
Robert Lisney
Indiana Lown-Collins
David Marks
Corinne Meredith
India Semper-Hughes
Harriet Varley**
Chair Emeritus
Richard Humphreys

POOR CLARE

Chiara Atik

Poor Clare was originally produced by the Echo Theater Company (Chris Fields, Artistic Director), Los Angeles, California, in October 2021. The cast was as follows:

CLARE	Jordan Hull
PEPPA	Martica De Cardenas
ALMA	Kari Lee Cartwright
BEATRICE	Donna Zadeh
BEGGAR	Tony DeCarlo
FRANCIS	Michael Sturgis
ORTOLANA	Ann Noble
SERVANT WOMAN	Trinity Catlin
UNDERSTUDY	Sam Morelos

Director	Alana Dietze
Set Designer	Amanda Knehans
Lighting Designer	Azra King-Abadi
Costume Designer	Dianne K. Graebner
Wig & Hair Designer	Klint Flowers
Sound Designer	Jeff Gardner
Production Stage Manager	Christopher Jerabek

Characters

CLARE
PEPPA
ALMA
BEATRICE
BEGGAR
FRANCIS
ORTOLANA
THE POOR

And SERVANT WOMEN

Note on Text

A double forward slash (//) indicates interrupted/overlapping speech.

This text went to press before the end of rehearsals and so may differ slightly from the play as performed.

ACT ONE

Scene One

Assisi (Italy), 1211.

CLARE, *eighteen, is sitting cross-legged on a wooden bench. Behind her, her two servants,* PEPPA *(fifties) and* ALMA *(thirties), are busily braiding her hair into one of those insanely complicated medieval hairstyles involving lots of loops and plaits.*

CLARE *is young, she's beautiful, she's Christian. She's like a contestant on* The Bachelor, *but not the dramatic villainous ones, but rather the nice, pretty ones who rub the backs of the girls who are crying.*

Life has been pretty good for her. She's got great hair.

She's cupping a chalice, from which she takes occasional sips. Maybe there's food on the table nearby from which she takes bites occasionally as she listens to PEPPA *and* ALMA *gossip.*

She yawns. It's early.

ALMA. I don't know that I have any good gossip. I'm trying to think.

PEPPA. Did you hear Guido Conti is back?

ALMA. No! When'd he get back?

PEPPA. Yesterday. Yesterday morning.

ALMA. Oh my god!

CLARE. Wait, who?

PEPPA. You know Ubaldo?

CLARE. No?

PEPPA. He works in the stables?

ALMA. Ubaldo!

CLARE. Does he have a beard?

ALMA. No, you're thinking of Renzo.

PEPPA. That's Renzo. Ubaldo is kind of heavier, a bit older, he's got a scar on his lip –

CLARE. Oh, yeah yeah yeah yeah.

ALMA. His tunic is red.

CLARE. Right, yes.

PEPPA. So Ubaldo's *son,* Guido, just got back from crusade.

CLARE. Oh my gosh!

ALMA. Did you see him? Does he look the same?

PEPPA. He looks exactly the same. Bit swarthier. We threw a little homecoming for him last night.

ALMA. Fun!!

PEPPA. The stable guys all pitched in and got a boar.

CLARE. Aw.

ALMA. That was sweet. Those guys are so sweet.

PEPPA. Yeah, they're a really good crew.

(*To* CLARE.) Bodkin?

CLARE *hands her a long, thin needle, which she's keeping in a pile in her lap.* PEPPA *expertly uses it to pin up a braid, then begins on another strand.*

ALMA. What's he gonna do now?

PEPPA. Well his dad was trying to convince him to take a week off, at least, re-acclimate –

ALMA. Sure.

PEPPA. But he was like 'no no', you know, doesn't wanna be a burden, so I think he was gonna go see today about a job. Probably in the stables.

ALMA. Awww, with his dad! That's really great. I'd been praying for him.

PEPPA. Yeah, everybody was!

CLARE. Did he say what it was like?

ALMA. Bodkin?

  CLARE *hands her one*.

CLARE. Did Guido say what the crusades were like?

PEPPA. He said he was very lucky not to get sick. I guess most
  people got sick?

ALMA. I've heard that!

PEPPA. What else... oh, well, he sailed obviously.

CLARE. Oh, wow, yeah.

PEPPA. They were on a ship for three weeks. OH! HE SAW
  A WHALE!

CLARE. Really??

ALMA. Stop!

PEPPA. That's what he said.

CLARE. How did he even know that that was what it was?

PEPPA. I think it's the type of thing that if you see one, there's
  no doubt what it is.

CLARE. Whoa.

PEPPA. Hair tie.

  CLARE *hands her a tiny leather strip from her lap*.

CLARE. Well, I'm really glad he's back safe but I have to say
  I'm very anti-crusade.

ALMA. I wouldn't mind seeing the sea.

CLARE. My mother's seen it! On her trips to the Holy Land.

ALMA. I didn't realize you cross a sea to get to the Holy Land!

CLARE. Yeah! I forget which but. You definitely go over the
  ocean for like a long time.

PEPPA. Your mom is brave.

CLARE. Yeah, totally. It sounds awful. I mean, she's glad she went. Like it's a good thing to do, going to the Holy Land. But it's like. So much work and money!!

ALMA. Hair tie.

CLARE hands her one.

CLARE. Like, even just to be gone that long is stressful and just. A big commitment! And you know, with my grandma getting older it's like, every time she sets off on a trip she doesn't know what she's coming home to. Which is so hard. I dunno, would you be able to just drop everything and leave for a year?

PEPPA (*with a glance towards* ALMA). Well, no.

ALMA. Definitely not.

CLARE. Right, yeah, me neither! It'd definitely be hard. And you have to bring *all* your own supplies, all your own food, because god knows what you'll find over there. It starts to add up! And you have to bring gifts for everyone you're going to meet. And like, nothing chintzy either, you need something really nice. Like a book or something.

PEPPA. Bodkin.

CLARE. And then *another* reason I'm like, not dying to go to the Holy Land even though I know it's like, a really good thing to do, is... they're not great with women over there.

ALMA. Really??

CLARE. *Yes*, and I find it pretty problematic. Like, they don't sequester women. My mom was just like, *out* in public. Like, out in the streets. *With the masses.* I mean she had bodyguards but that's it.

She holds out her hands in front of her to demonstrate space.

Here's my mom, and *here's* the general public. It's like. *Not* safe for women.

ALMA. Wow.

PEPPA. Bodkin.

ALMA. It's so weird because it's like. The Holy Land.

CLARE. I know.

ALMA. Like you'd think it would be more…

CLARE. I know. My mom's my hero.

PEPPA (*to* ALMA). I'm done on my side.

ALMA. Sorry, yeah, almost.

ALMA *begins braiding faster.*

CLARE. I *do* think I'll probably go some day. Just 'cause I think it's important to like, push yourself for your faith. And I want to be a good Christian and obviously a big part of that is going to the Holy Land. But. I'm not exactly looking forward to it.

Her sister, BEATRICE, *enters. Her hair has also been done up in an extraordinarily complicated style.*

BEATRICE. You're still not done??

CLARE. Almost. Oh my god! You look so cute!

BEATRICE. I know, they did a good job today.

CLARE. Wait come here, let me look at you.

BEATRICE. Look at the loop in the back.

CLARE. It's super-cute, I really like it.

PEPPA *pins up* CLARE'*s last braid.*

PEPPA. Alright. All done.

CLARE. Oh! –

BEATRICE. Oh, cool. It looks cool, Clare.

CLARE. Yeah?

She reaches her hand up to feel her hair.

It feels cool!

BEATRICE. Yeah, I love it. I'm getting that tomorrow.

PEPPA. Shake.

> CLARE *shakes her head up and down and around. The braids stay put.*

> Does your head hurt? Too tight?

CLARE. It's fine! Is this side even? I can't tell if it's higher.

ALMA. I think you're good –

PEPPA. Let me see –

BEATRICE. Mom wants to get there early to talk to the bishop.

CLARE. Will you tell her I'm coming? I just need to get my breviary.

BEATRICE. Okay, we're in the courtyard waiting.

> BEATRICE *exits.*

CLARE. Wait, Beatrice!

> BEATRICE *enters again.*

> Do you like this dress?

BEATRICE. Ya.

CLARE. Okay. I'll be right there.

> BEATRICE *exits again.*

> I don't think I need the hot-water bottle tonight. I was too warm last night.

PEPPA. It's supposed to get cool again tonight.

CLARE. Oh, really?

PEPPA. I can prepare it just in case but you don't have to use it.

CLARE. Okay, I was just saying in case it's less work for you.

PEPPA. A hot-water bottle's no work. (*Finishing the hair.*) Alright that should hold!

CLARE. You guys! Thank you!

PEPPA. You look adorable.

ALMA. It's super-cute.

CLARE. Are you guys heading to services?

ALMA. We went before.

CLARE. Oh my god, so early! Good for you. Okay, I'm off, then! Love you guys!! Oh say hi to Guido!! And welcome home!! From me!!

ALMA *and* PEPPA *bow deeply as* CLARE *rushes out of the room.*

Scene Two

CLARE *and* BEATRICE *stroll home from church. Unseen by them, sitting on the ground is a* BEGGAR.

BEATRICE. Okay so for the skirt, I'm thinking like a gold thread, and then the cloth would be like... I don't know, I'm thinking purple...

CLARE. 'Kay.

BEATRICE. Or like... purplish blue...

CLARE. Indigo?

BEATRICE. Something in the purplish-blue family. A purplish-blue, kinda flowy skirt with gold thread.

CLARE. I like that 'cause it's like... deferential.

BEATRICE. What do you mean?

CLARE. Blue is like, modest. It's like what Mary wore.

BEATRICE. Well, wait.

CLARE. Uh-oh.

BEATRICE. For the bodice... like I want it to go to here-ish –

She gestures to her collarbone.

Very covered up, very classy.

CLARE. 'Kay…

BEATRICE. In red.

CLARE. No.

BEATRICE. Just like, a cute lil red bodice.

CLARE. I don't want to not be supportive – but no.

BEATRICE. That's my vision!

CLARE. Beatrice! No! That is not appropriate.

BEATRICE. Why?

CLARE. *Red?* Mom would never let you.

BEATRICE. She might!

CLARE. You are fifteen!

BEATRICE. So? Mom was married at fifteen.

CLARE. Yeah, and A: that was disgusting, and B: when you're
married you can wear whatever you want, obviously.

BEATRICE. And I'm never gonna *get* married if I don't show
a little. Spark!

CLARE. What are you *talking* about?

BEATRICE. I'm just saying, we don't have that many
opportunities to like –

CLARE. To what?

BEATRICE. To like *attract suitors*.

CLARE. Oh my god. You should not be worrying about this
right now!!

BEATRICE. I'm not *worried* about it, I'm just saying. I gotta
like.

CLARE.…what?

BEATRICE. Show people the light's on at the inn, if you catch my drift. I am open for business.

CLARE. I think you're too boy-crazy.

BEATRICE. I'm really not.

CLARE. You *think* about them too much. Like, there are other things in the world, Bea!

BEATRICE. Easy for you to say!

CLARE.... We don't know that.

BEATRICE (*rolling her eyes*). Oh my god. She *said* she found you the perfect suitor, he's coming *to dinner*, why would he be coming *to dinner* if they hadn't already agreed on a –

CLARE. Don't jinx me!! We don't know!

BEATRICE. Okay. Just. I thought the red bodice would be cute, and if someone nice were to see me walking to church and think so, too, that wouldn't be the end of the world.

CLARE. It honestly worries me that this is how you view relationships between men and women.

BEATRICE. Oh, you're such an expert.

CLARE. I'm just saying. That kind of point of view is not going to set you up for future happiness. Attracting someone has nothing to do with what you wear, and everything to do with inner confidence.

BEATRICE. Well then I'm fucked.

CLARE *stops walking, and faces* BEATRICE, *earnestly.*

Oh god. I was joking.

CLARE. Bea. Listen to me.

BEATRICE. *I was joking*, you don't have to –

CLARE. You have every reason to feel confident around men.

BEATRICE. Not really!

CLARE. Yes, you do! Don't talk down about yourself like that! Seriously! Repeat after me. I am wealthy.

BEATRICE *rolls her eyes*.

Say it!

BEATRICE. I am wealthy.

CLARE. I am pious.

BEATRICE *laughs*.

You are. You *are*. You pray!

BEATRICE. I mean I say the words?

CLARE. 'I am pious.'

BEATRICE. I'm pious.

CLARE. I am in possession of a sizable dowry…

BEATRICE. I am in possession of a sizable dowry…

CLARE. And any man in the kingdom would be lucky to have me.

BEATRICE. And any man in the kingdom would be lucky to have me.

CLARE. Yes!

BEATRICE. Eugh.

CLARE. I really wasn't confident at your age, either, but saying these little mantras can really help. It's like fake it till you make it.

BEATRICE (*pouting*). Well now I don't know what dress to have made-uh.

CLARE. Okay, we said indigo skirt.

BEATRICE. Yeah.

CLARE. Okay, okay, what about like a green? Like a green brocade?

BEATRICE. I don't think brocade would really go with the white-fur trim I'm supposed to use.

CLARE. Okay, what if... I lent you my ermine.

BEATRICE. Really??

CLARE. You CANNOT GET IT MUDDY though.

BEATRICE. I won't. Oh my god, I won't, I promise, I'll be so careful –

CLARE. I love that fucking ermine more than you and if anything happens I'll have you skinned and wear you for gloves.

BEATRICE. Jesus.

CLARE. Just saying.

BEATRICE. You're gonna be married in like a month and your husband is gonna buy you a thousand ermines –

CLARE. WE DON'T KNOW THAT.

BEATRICE. Okay. I'll be so careful. I really promise. If it rains I'll have two servants carry the train –

CLARE. If it rains I'm not lending it to you!!

BEATRICE. Fine. Of course. Yes. Deal.

CLARE. I don't know what I'm gonna do about *my* wardrobe. It might not make sense for me to have dresses ordered until I know whether I'm going to need a –

The BEGGAR, *who has been sitting quietly asleep and unseen throughout this whole conversation, suddenly reaches out to them.*

BEGGAR. Could you help me get something to eat?

CLARE *and* BEATRICE *scream, completely startled, and run to the other side of the stage. They double over, laughing, exhilarated – the kind of 'egging each other on' people sometimes do when they've been startled.*

CLARE. OH. MY –

BEATRICE. That scared the SHIT out of me –

CLARE. I had *no idea* there was a *person* there –

BEATRICE. I didn't see anyone!! I thought it was like, a literal pile of garbage –

CLARE. I like, can't breathe.

BEATRICE. Oh my god.

CLARE. I like. Screamed.

BEATRICE. I. *Screamed!*

CLARE. Oh my god. Were they there the whole time?

BEATRICE. My heart is like, still racing.

CLARE. Oh my god.

They look at each other and laugh.

Scene Three

Another morning.

PEPPA *and* ALMA *are deep in a whispered conversation.*

CLARE *enters, her hair loose and past her waist. She's holding a chalice, a little bleary.*

CLARE. Morning!

PEPPA *and* ALMA *bow.*

PEPPA. Good morning.

ALMA. Morning.

CLARE *takes a seat in the chair in front of them. They begin brushing her hair.*

CLARE. Can we do like, a bun in the back with those two loopy things on the side?

PEPPA. Of course.

PEPPA and ALMA begin to section off hair. CLARE settles into her seat. Takes a sip of drink.

CLARE. How are you guys today? What's going on?

ALMA. Okay, so, you haven't heard.

CLARE. Heard what?

PEPPA. Alma...

CLARE. You guys. What.

ALMA. This guy...

She starts giggling.

PEPPA. This... young... youth... had a little moment in market square yesterday.

ALMA. He stripped naked.

CLARE. What??

ALMA. In front of everybody.

CLARE. Oh my god, what is HAPPENING? I feel like it must be a full moon or something. Yesterday there was this lunatic in the courtyard when my sister and I were walking, now this?

PEPPA. The world is going to hell, that's for sure.

CLARE. Were you there?

PEPPA. No, but my cousin was.

ALMA. I just missed it by like, a *second*. When I arrived they had just dragged him away.

CLARE. Just like, a crazy person?? I mean obviously a crazy person.

PEPPA. Poor thing.

ALMA. His dad's a silk merchant.

CLARE. What's his name?

ALMA. Francis. Know him?

CLARE. No.

ALMA. We haven't told you the craziest part.

CLARE. What?

ALMA. He did it *in front of the bishop*.

CLARE. WHAT?

ALMA. Swear.

CLARE. What is WRONG with people?

PEPPA. How much time do you have?

CLARE. What did the bishop do?

ALMA. He took off his own cloak and covered him.

CLARE. Wow. Good for the bishop.

PEPPA. Can you imagine being in the market, minding your own business, and then *that* happens?

ALMA. I almost was!! I missed it by like, a minute!

PEPPA. What would you have done?

CLARE. Screamed. I would have screamed.

ALMA. I don't know!

PEPPA. I think he must be really disturbed. He was ranting and raving when they took him away.

CLARE. Like about the devil and stuff?

PEPPA. About the poor.

ALMA. Oh god, I heard that. That was so weird.

CLARE. The poor?

PEPPA. The whole thing was a protest.

CLARE. Against poor people?

PEPPA. Against *poverty*.

CLARE. Like the concept of poverty?

PEPPA. He's 'anti'.

CLARE. That's so dumb.

ALMA. Gosh.

CLARE. Like who is *pro*-poverty? It's just a thing. Like just a fact. Of life.

PEPPA. He thinks we're all just ignoring it.

CLARE. !! We're not!!

ALMA. No one's ignoring it.

PEPPA. All the, you know. The beggars that we have in town now.

CLARE. Well, we've always had peasants.

PEPPA. That's not the same.

ALMA. That's not the same thing.

PEPPA. He's talking about – well maybe you haven't noticed but there are –

CLARE. No, I know –

PEPPA. *Tons* moving in –

CLARE. Yeah, I know what you're talking about. It's sad.

ALMA. I get really upset about it.

PEPPA. He thinks we're not doing enough. I guess.

CLARE. Well, what is taking all your clothes off supposed to do? Like, I'm sure the poor are so grateful that he just mooned the bishop.

ALMA. Ha!

CLARE. I'm sure that really keeps them warm at night.

Beat.

PEPPA. Yeah I mean I think it's more about renouncing his
    father's wealth. His father's wealth paid for his clothes. So he
    doesn't want them any more. He 'cast them off'.

ALMA. His father's a silk merchant. Bet those were some nice
    pantaloons he flung in the mud!

CLARE. I just don't get how he thinks any of it is like. Helping.

ALMA. There are better ways to help the poor!

CLARE. Right!

ALMA. Like, alms. And like.

CLARE. Soup kitchens.

ALMA. Yes.

CLARE. My family throws a three-day feast every year on my
    uncle's name day. It's like three days of food, we feed
    everyone.

PEPPA. We know!

ALMA. It's really nice!

CLARE. We don't turn anyone away. It's like, three guaranteed
    hot meals. With meat!

ALMA. Not everyone does that.

CLARE. It's a lot of work but we're happy to do it. It means
    a lot to us.

PEPPA. Of course.

ALMA. It's so great.

PEPPA. I think it's good for everyone to do everything they can.

ALMA. I agree.

CLARE. Yeah. It's really important.

    PEPPA *and* ALMA *braid silently.* CLARE *contemplates.*

    I mean, yeah, it's crazy. There are a lot of really desperate
    people right now, it's horrible. It's a horrible political
    climate. We should all be pitching in.

PEPPA. Yeah.

ALMA. Yeah.

CLARE. I just don't really get why this guy thinks taking his clothes off is the best way to help. Also, not to be that person, but a woman would never do something like that.

PEPPA. Never.

ALMA. So true.

CLARE. Because women are *rational*.

PEPPA. Amen.

ALMA *and* PEPPA *braid. After a beat:*

CLARE. I wonder if the bishop got his cloak back.

Scene Four

The town square.

FRANCIS, *an eccentric-looking man dressed in a bright-blue robe and leaning on a wooden staff, holds a basket full of food with a big conspicuous bow tied on it.*

CLARE *stands across from him, smiling.*

CLARE. I feel like we *must* have met at some point.

FRANCIS. Yeah, I dunno…

CLARE. Or at least have friends in common. Do you ever hang out with the Menotti brothers?

FRANCIS. Nope.

CLARE. What about Nello Briziarelli?

FRANCIS. I know who that is, but I've never met him.

CLARE. Greco Ferrante?

FRANCIS. Nope.

CLARE. Oh my gosh! He's like really tall, he was like, the *hero* when the Germans were trying to invade, he won like six battles or something, everyone's obsessed with him.

FRANCIS *shrugs*.

It's such a small town! There's no way our paths haven't crossed.

FRANCIS. I dunno! I've been really doing my own thing lately, so.

CLARE. Okay, just one more, last one:

FRANCIS. Okay.

CLARE. DID you go to the palio last year?

FRANCIS. Only 'cause my dad's really into it.

CLARE. Okay, do you play?

FRANCIS. No.

CLARE. Okay, well, at last year's palio, you know the girl who gave the wreath of flowers to the winning team?

FRANCIS. Uhm…

CLARE. You watched the game.

FRANCIS. Kind of?

CLARE. Okay, and then after the game did you watch the presentation to the winners?

FRANCIS. I mean I must have, I just don't really remember –

CLARE. This girl had a *huge* wreath of roses that she put around the horse's neck? And she had plaited her hair with the same roses used in the wreath, so her hair kinda looked like a wreath too? Do you remember that?

FRANCIS. Vaguely?

CLARE. THAT'S ME!! That was me.

FRANCIS. Oh. Okay, cool.

CLARE. So you *have* seen me before!

FRANCIS. I don't remember, but I guess so.

CLARE. I knew it, it's too small of a town for us to be complete strangers to one another. I like your robe!

FRANCIS. What?

CLARE. Your robe. Very striking.

FRANCIS. Oh. That's not really the point of it.

CLARE. Oh. Right, no.

FRANCIS. I just mean. That's not why I wear it.

CLARE. I was just –

FRANCIS. // I don't want to be wearing something that people feel the need to compliment.

CLARE. Oh, sure.

FRANCIS. Like I don't want people to focus on what I'm wearing. I just wanna blend in.

CLARE. You don't.

FRANCIS. Okay…

CLARE. I don't think that's a bad thing, though!

FRANCIS. Well I don't want people to look at me and think 'cool robe'!

CLARE. I don't think anyone is going to look at you and think 'cool robe'; I just think it's a nice color on you.

FRANCIS *sighs, impatiently.*

Oh my god, just, take a compliment!

FRANCIS. Okay. Thank you for the compliment. And thank you for the bread basket. Is there anything else I can do for you?

CLARE. Actually… Well basically, I wanted to come here because I'm honestly really curious and was wondering if you could tell me a little bit about your whole deal.

FRANCIS. Oh!

CLARE. Like your whole thing, what is your whole thing, that you're doing. Is that okay to ask?

FRANCIS. YES!

CLARE. Okay, good. I wasn't sure!

FRANCIS. I will literally tell anyone who asks what my deal is. I'm like, trying to shout it on the streets. It's not a secret. Most people don't want to know.

CLARE. I do!!

FRANCIS. Okay. It's really simple. I want to radically upend the financial structures of our society and redistribute wealth.

CLARE.… haha. Whoa!

FRANCIS. Right?

CLARE. Yeah.

FRANCIS. Maybe 'redistribute wealth' is the wrong way of putting it. I don't want to take money away from rich people to make other rich people. I just wanna make it so there are *no* rich people any more.

CLARE. Wow.

FRANCIS. I don't know if you've noticed, but – What's your name again?

CLARE. Clare.

FRANCIS. Clare, I don't know if you've noticed, but the distribution of wealth right now is insanely unequal, like, insanely.

    CLARE *nods*.

CLARE. I've heard that.

FRANCIS. And the way things are structured right now, that wealth gap is just going to get bigger. We live in a system where children of wealthy people are going to just get wealthier and wealthier. I mean, you, Clare, were born rich –

CLARE. Oh, we're not rich! We're comfortable.

FRANCIS. Do your parents own your palazzo on the piazza?

CLARE. It's not really a palazzo, it's more just a big house.

FRANCIS. Do you own it?

CLARE. It was my grandfather's, we didn't like, *buy* it.

FRANCIS. Okay, how 'bout this: when your dad goes to battle –

CLARE. We live with my uncle.

FRANCIS. When your uncle goes to battle does he march under your family banner or a different family's banner?

CLARE. Our own crest.

FRANCIS. You're rich. You're rich! The first step is just admitting it.

CLARE. Okay. I admit it.

FRANCIS. It's not your fault! It's not anything you did bad, it's just you, like me, were born into a life of privilege you neither deserve nor earned.

CLARE. Sure.

FRANCIS. So why do you *get* that? Why do you get servants and rooms and dresses and someone to change your chamberpots and prepare hot meals for you? Why do you get that and others get *nothing*?

CLARE. Well. I mean, if you're asking literally, I think it's because my family fought for the land back during the Visigoth –

FRANCIS. That's your *family*. That was your grandfather, your great-grandfather. What did *you* do?

CLARE. Like me personally? Directly or indirectly? 'Cause I guess, directly, nothing, but indirectly, I go to church. And I sew tapestries and watch my little cousins and I *read* which not a lot of women can say –

FRANCIS. You don't shovel snow. You don't shovel shit. You don't scrub floors. You don't scrub pots for hours and hours and hours a day until your back breaks.

CLARE. Well, no –

FRANCIS. I'm not saying this is your fault!

CLARE. Okay.

FRANCIS. I'm just saying. You're pretty lucky.

CLARE. I know! I try really hard to be aware of it. And be grateful. And to give back.

FRANCIS. 'Give back.' It's not giving back when the people you're giving to never had any of it in the first place. So I'm just renouncing all of that. I want no part in wealth I didn't earn.

CLARE. So... aren't you just sort of. Martyring yourself? For no reason? I'm just asking!

FRANCIS. It's not no reason. Things have gotten bad, people are really struggling!

CLARE. No, I know that.

FRANCIS. I've been around a lot of devastation, especially in the last month. Especially in the encampments. Crying children, starving children, freezing children –

CLARE. Yes I am aware. It's sad.

FRANCIS. It's sad. But no one's doing anything about it. Because at the end of the day, no one is willing to go with less so that other people can have more. Except for me. I'm willing to do that.

CLARE. That's your thing.

FRANCIS. That's my thing.

CLARE. Wow.

Beat.

I still don't totally get what you're going to *do*.

FRANCIS. What do you mean?

CLARE. Like I get your philosophy. But other than taking a stand, and handing out bread, what are you *doing*? You need to put your energy somewhere, you need like a *project*.

FRANCIS. My project is to devote myself to a life of prayer and benefaction.

CLARE. But like, in addition.

FRANCIS. Kinda think that's a big project!

CLARE. Alright. Well. Very interesting. Good luck.

FRANCIS. Thanks for the bread basket.

CLARE. The little round ones – wait –

She rifles through the bread basket for a second, pulling out a small roll.

These are so good. I mean they're all good, our baker is amazing. But these are *so* good.

FRANCIS. I'm sure they'll be appreciated.

CLARE. One thing though. How did you know our house was on the piazza? You asked whether we owned the house on the piazza. You knew the specific house. You knew exactly who I was when I walked in here. You're not as removed from town gossip as you think. The first step is just admitting it.

She exits.

Scene Five

CLARE *and* BEATRICE *walk home from church.*

BEATRICE. He seems nice.

CLARE. Yeah.

BEATRICE. Like, I didn't really talk to him, obviously, but. Seems like a nice guy.

CLARE. Uh-huh. I think so.

Beat.

BEATRICE. And it's cool about the cheese festival.

CLARE. What?

BEATRICE. What he said about that cheese festival? Like the whole town gets together on the day the cheeses are ready? That seems fun.

CLARE. Oh. Yeah.

BEATRICE. Definitely visiting you for that.

CLARE. Please!

BEATRICE. I will!

Beat.

CLARE. I think his house sounds really impressive.

BEATRICE. Yeah!

CLARE. It's cool that I'd have like. A sister-in-law.

BEATRICE. Yeah, that's nice, that was not a given.

CLARE. No.

I will say…

He's a little older than I expected.

BEATRICE. Okay, I wasn't going to say anything, but… yeah.

CLARE. Like, *what*?

BEATRICE. Yeah, I don't know.

CLARE. Is Mom insane?

BEATRICE. Yeah, like… does she realize?

CLARE. Is she just setting me up with who SHE would like to be with?

BEATRICE. I don't know. It honestly seems kind of crazy.

CLARE. But the house seems great.

BEATRICE. No, I'm jealous about the house.

And it kinda seemed like he'd be off fighting a lot.

CLARE. Yeah, it did seem that way, didn't it?

BEATRICE. I mean, he said! 'These days, the only way to not be invaded – '

CLARE. ' – is to do the invading', yeah that was a little aggro, no?

BEATRICE. But practical!

CLARE. I guess.

BEATRICE. I mean, he hasn't been invaded!

CLARE. No.

BEATRICE. I think, realistically, he's gonna be home three months out of the year. And the rest of the time you're gonna have the place to yourself.

CLARE. Yeah.

BEATRICE. So that'll be great!

BEGGAR (*without really looking up*). Spare some change?

BEATRICE. When you think about it, it could have actually been a whole lot worse. And I'll come visit you. For the cheese festival!

CLARE. Right. Yes.

BEATRICE. Have you thought about your trousseau?

CLARE. Yeah, I've started to.

BEATRICE. What are you thinking?

CLARE. Well, I guess it depends on the wedding. Whatever's practical. Probably a new travelling outfit...

The pair walk offstage. After a bit, CLARE comes back. Approaches the BEGGAR.

BEGGAR. Spare some change?

CLARE dumps a few coins into the BEGGAR's outstretched hand and hurries away.

Thank you – whoa –

He looks up, shocked.

Miss! Wait!

CLARE turns, keeping her distance.

Thank you. Thank you so much.

CLARE. No – it's nothing –

BEGGAR. Really. Thank you.

CLARE. It's nothing.

BEGGAR. *Thank* you.

Uncomfortable, CLARE *turns and exits.*

Scene Six

CLARE, BEATRICE *and their mother,* ORTOLANA, *sit in chairs, with their feet in basins of water. Below them, three* SERVANT WOMEN *wash their feet. Unlike her daughters,* ORTOLANA*'s hair is completely covered.*

CLARE. Wait, can I ask something random?

BEATRICE. Always.

CLARE. Are we – would you guys consider us rich?

BEATRICE. Ooh, interesting question.

ORTOLANA. Clare. Come on.

CLARE. What?

ORTOLANA. That's just not. A nice thing to talk about.

BEATRICE. Mom, you talk about who's rich all the time!

CLARE. Why is it not a nice thing to talk about?

ORTOLANA. No, I do not.

BEATRICE. Are you kidding? // Yes, you do.

CLARE. Yeah, you actually do.

ORTOLANA (*to the* SERVANT). The water's just a little bit hot for me, thank you so much.

The SERVANT *nods and gets up.*

BEATRICE. You're always like 'That family's richer than God.' 'Her dad is supposed to be *so* rich.'

ORTOLANA. I don't believe in talking about money too much.

BEATRICE. // 'That family used to be rich, but now they're not.'

ORTOLANA. *Okay*, Beatrice.

CLARE. But if someone asked you, 'Are you rich?' what would you say?

ORTOLANA. I would say 'That's an invasive question and I don't feel comfortable answering it.'

CLARE. Just answer the question.

ORTOLANA. I don't know!

We are very fortunate.

BEATRICE. That doesn't really answer her question.

CLARE. That's not an answer.

ORTOLANA. We're fortunate! We're a lucky family!

I think we're smart about money.

It's not so much how big your fortune is as how well you manage it.

BEATRICE. So we have a fortune.

ORTOLANA. Well, sure, but. A fortune can be any amount. I have a fortune in daughters.

CLARE. Don't you think that like, within our town, we're among the most well-off.

ORTOLANA. Not compared to the Portenzas!!

BEATRICE. What about the Portenzas?

CLARE. Other than them.

ORTOLANA. The Portenzas are richer than God.

BEATRICE. They've got two stables…

ORTOLANA. There's a petition going around to rename the town Portenza.

CLARE. Literally anyone else other than the Portenzas!

ORTOLANA. I don't know…

BEATRICE (*glancing down at her foot*). Oh… do I have a little –

BEATRICE *leans over to inspect her foot.*

CLARE. Like if the Portenzas were wiped out by plague *tomorrow*, the whole family, then we would be the richest family in town, we just *would*.

ORTOLANA. I guess so.

BEATRICE (*aside, to her* SERVANT). It's like… a little callus or something? Do you feel?

The SERVANT *feels.*

CLARE. That's all I'm trying to say.

ORTOLANA. But that's just Assisi. I mean over in Perugia there are like twenty families twice as rich as the Portenzas.

CLARE. Well, I'm sure.

BEATRICE (*to her* SERVANT). Does it come off if you scrub?

ORTOLANA. And elsewhere! I mean! Riches you can't even imagine, Clare. These people have *castles*. These people have *armies*. The little Sforza girls get jewels before they cut their teeth. They cut their teeth *on* jewels.

BEATRICE (*to her* SERVANT). I guess just kinda work around it?

ORTOLANA. You don't even get ermines until your eighteenth birthdays, and that's like. That's an extravagance! I mean, your world-views are pretty provincial right now but some day you'll travel and you'll realize that you don't even know the *meaning* of rich, I mean not even a whiff of it.

BEATRICE (*to her* SERVANT). Yeah that works. Thank you!

CLARE. But I'm not talking about the rest of the world, I'm literally just talking about Assisi, and our life, and the people we know. And in terms of that scale *someone* has to be rich, *someone* has to be poor. We're *not* poor. Right?

ORTOLANA. Obviously.

CLARE. I think we're rich.

ORTOLANA. I just wouldn't go that far.

BEATRICE. Why is it such a big deal to admit to being rich?

ORTOLANA. It's not a big deal, it's just not *accurate*.

CLARE. You *just* said –

ORTOLANA. Why don't you just save us all time and tell us what you're digging at?

CLARE. I'm not digging –

ORTOLANA. Yes you're clawing at something and you're gonna just keep clawing at us until you get it. Just spit it out.

CLARE. I think we're rich is all I'm saying.

BEATRICE. But do you *want* us to be rich?

CLARE. No, I don't care, I just want us to admit we are.

BEATRICE. I admit it?

CLARE. Mom doesn't. It doesn't square away with her super-pious self-image.

ORTOLANA. What does being rich have to do with being pious?

CLARE. I'm just saying!

ORTOLANA. You can be rich and pious. Look at the pope! And I'll have you know I've worked really hard for what I have. Which means I've really worked hard for what *you* have. You could be grateful.

BEATRICE. Everyone just needs to take a deep breath.

ORTOLANA. I'm just saying. That dowry got you a pretty good match.

CLARE. I know. I'm happy about that! It's just that I've been thinking.

ORTOLANA. Okay…

CLARE. I think we could do a little more to give. I just mean we're lucky and maybe we could be doing more for people who aren't as fortunate as we are.

ORTOLANA. Is that what this is all about? Clare! Obviously I love that. I'm on board with that! I'm really impressed that that's where your head is. That makes me feel like I did my job right. Like I'm raising you girls right.

BEATRICE. Are you thinking, like a clothes drive?

CLARE. Sure.

ORTOLANA. Oh, a clothes drive is a great idea. We have so much leftover fabric from St Swithin's, too. That's really really thoughtful.

CLARE. Great. That'll be great.

The WOMEN *sit in silent for a moment. The* SERVANTS *at their feet continue to scrub.*

BEATRICE. Oooooh! Did you guys hear about the guy who stripped in front of the bishop?

ORTOLANA. No, what are you talking about?

BEATRICE. Oh my god, Mom, it's. So insane.

Scene Seven

A tiny, falling-down church in the outskirts of town.

CLARE *enters, carefully stepping over old stones and construction debris. She approaches* FRANCIS, *who is cutting wood to make scaffolding. He's now wearing a brown robe.*

CLARE. Oooooooh. New robe!!!

FRANCIS. Oh. Hi.

CLARE. I like it. It's eccentric but not in a flashy way.

FRANCIS. Who told you I was out here?

CLARE. I think everyone knows you're squatting here...

FRANCIS. It's not really squatting when it's the house of God.

CLARE. But you're living here?

FRANCIS. Just while I fix it up.

CLARE. Welllllll, I heard the bishop's gonna try and kick
you out.

FRANCIS stops what he's doing and looks at her, alarmed.

FRANCIS. On what grounds?!

CLARE. On the grounds that you're weirdly renovating a church
that isn't yours?

FRANCIS. Why does he care? He let it go to shit to begin with.

CLARE. Only since he built the new one in the square!

FRANCIS. I hate that church.

CLARE. No you don't. Come on.

FRANCIS. I do!

CLARE. But it's beautiful! And so much closer to everything!
And has the cushioned pews!

FRANCIS. We already had plenty of churches in town.

CLARE. Not with cushioned pews!

FRANCIS. Waste of money.

CLARE. It's so roomy, it fits the whole town.

FRANCIS. Fits way more than the whole town, that's why it's
so ridiculous.

CLARE. I mean I know you're probably right but I still love it.
And it's like. Good for the town and stuff.

He looks at her and laughs.

FRANCIS. How is it good for the town?

CLARE. Brings in pilgrims? I dunno. Civic pride.

*She walks around the perimeter of the church, stepping over
debris.*

So what are you gonna do with this place?

FRANCIS. Bolster the walls, new ceiling beams. Paint job.

CLARE. Cool.

FRANCIS. What I'd really love is to get someone in to do frescos –

CLARE. Cool!!

FRANCIS. I know. It's so expensive though. I gotta find someone who'd be willing to do it for free as sort of a donation thing. My DREAM, which probably won't happen but, if we're talking just, total fantasy terms, not getting into logistics at all –

CLARE. Sure –

FRANCIS. But my DREAM would be to do basically all of Genesis on *this* wall, then the Annunciation/Nativity moving up towards the nave –

CLARE. Wow –

FRANCIS. And then end with the Passion like, up at the altar.

CLARE. That's so cool.

FRANCIS. Yeah?

CLARE. Yeah, I think that's really cool. I think you should make it happen.

FRANCIS. I mean I don't know if it's even practical in terms of space… and Genesis seems sort of hard to depict.

CLARE. But maybe an artist could have like, a cool approach –

FRANCIS. Maybe.

CLARE. Or maybe you just start with the Annunciation right away.

FRANCIS (*nodding*). I could.

CLARE. Yeah.

FRANCIS. Yeah. 'Cause it's actually not that big a space. So if we did that, we could move the Annunciation right to –

FRANCIS *trips*.

CLARE. Whoops –

FRANCIS. I keep tripping on my robe.

CLARE. Yeah, you need like a belt or something. Do you have a belt?

FRANCIS. No. I renounced all my accessories –

CLARE. Right, duh. Well do you have like string or –

FRANCIS. Uhm –

CLARE. Like a rope or something?

FRANCIS. There's this rope?

CLARE. Oh that'll totally work. Just tie it around, like that –

She ties the rope around his waist.

How's that?

FRANCIS. That's great. That helps. Thanks.

CLARE (*back to the church*). So once you get it all fixed up, then what happens to it?

FRANCIS. Then ideally it's open seven days a week, matins and vespers, for all of lower town.

CLARE. I think that's really nice. I just.

FRANCIS. What?

CLARE. Just, the bishop seemed pretty intent on not letting this happen!

FRANCIS. I bet it's not even the bishop. I bet it's my fucking dad acting through the bishop.

CLARE. The bishop isn't a puppet.

FRANCIS. Is that a joke? Of course the bishop is a puppet.

CLARE. I don't really think you're being fair right now.

FRANCIS. How am I not being fair??

CLARE. The church *is* under his jurisdiction and you *are* squatting in it and like, planning frescos. Without asking.

FRANCIS. I'm *renovating* –

CLARE. Yeah I'm not saying you shouldn't, I'm just saying, technically it's not yours and maybe if you *got permission*, like talked to the bishop, no one would have a problem with it.

FRANCIS. You're such a little rule-follower.

CLARE. No.

FRANCIS. But maybe I'll try it your way. Ask for permission.

CLARE. I just think that would be polite.

FRANCIS. I'll write to the Vatican right now.

CLARE. You're asking *the pope*? Like the actual pope?

FRANCIS. He's got ultimate jurisdiction.

CLARE. Yeah but. Does he *care*?

FRANCIS. The pope of all people *should* care. He's the representative of God on earth, isn't he?

CLARE. But so is the bishop! He *is*!

FRANCIS. If the pope says no, I'll leave. If the pope says yes, then the bishop certainly won't have a problem with it.

CLARE. I guess I'm just. Surprised by the order you're doing things, that's all.

FRANCIS. That's 'cause you're a product of the social order you grew up in. Not your fault. You just have to get it out of your head that one person is better than another person.

He goes back to writing his letter.

CLARE. Well. I've been thinking about that more, lately. My position. My privilege or whatever. And I've been really inspired to like. To *give* more.

FRANCIS. Uh-huh.

CLARE. So like, for example, I've just organized this clothing drive? At first it was just going to be me and my sisters and my mom, but then it kind of took on a life of its own, which is really cool, and actually now I'd say most of the noblewomen in town have gotten involved. And everyone is being really generous and like, donating a ton of clothes. Which is really exciting. How the whole community has sort of come together.

She waits for him to say something. He doesn't. So she presses on.

So anyway, we've collected like, a ton of clothes, like I said. So I wanted to talk to you about potentially dropping them off here.

FRANCIS. Why here?

CLARE. To donate them.

FRANCIS. I don't need clothes.

CLARE. No I mean! So you can distribute them. Like the bread basket!

FRANCIS. Why don't you just distribute them yourself?

CLARE. Oh. Uhm...

FRANCIS. You don't need me to donate to the poor.

She laughs.

CLARE....I mean I kind of do!

FRANCIS. No you don't.

CLARE. Well I don't know the best channels –

FRANCIS. The best channels would just be you giving these clothes to the people who need them.

CLARE. Okay but how do I know who needs it? And where do I go?

FRANCIS. You know the encampment under the Ponte Vecchio?

CLARE. Yeah...

FRANCIS. It's like twenty families right there. You could start there.

CLARE (*in a small voice*). Yeah, I guess.

   Beat.

   But. What do I do, just. Go up to someone and be like.
   'Excuse me, are you poor?' I mean, I can't do that! That's so –

FRANCIS. What?

CLARE. It's like, presumptuous!

FRANCIS. They live under a bridge! They know you know
   they're poor!

CLARE. I kinda just thought you would know people who you
   could give it to.

FRANCIS. I do. The encampment under Ponte Vecchio.

CLARE. It just seems really intense for ME to like –

   She shakes her head.

   I don't know. I know it sounds silly. But it feels intense to
   like. And I don't want to offend and –

FRANCIS. If you want to help people you gotta at least be able
   to acknowledge them.

CLARE. I know, I'm not trying to not –

FRANCIS. Are you scared?

   She hesitates.

CLARE. Only because of my social anxiety.

FRANCIS. I used to be really scared of lepers.

CLARE. Okay?

FRANCIS. I'd hear the bell around their neck and just.
   Sometimes I'd literally like, go down a different street, just
   like, out of my way to avoid having to look.

CLARE. I mean I'm still scared of lepers.

FRANCIS. I'm not anymore! That's my point. Because one
   night, I was walking around by myself outside the walls –

CLARE. Why?

FRANCIS. I was praying, actually –

CLARE. Weird –

FRANCIS. I actually like praying outdoors.

CLARE. But why at night?

FRANCIS. Oh I literally only sleep like four hours a night.

CLARE. What??

FRANCIS. Not out of zealotry, that's just always been my body clock.

CLARE. Wow.

FRANCIS. So I take walks and pray at night, because why not. So I'm walking through a field, thinking about God and just trying to practice gratitude. And I hear… a leper's bell.

CLARE. Ahhhh!

FRANCIS. Again: I'm in a field. It's moonlit. There's *no one* else around. No buildings to duck into, no streets to turn down – I hear *clang clang. Clang clang. Clang clang.*

CLARE. I have goosebumps. Look.

FRANCIS. The bell is getting louder and I can see this shrouded figure approaching and every instinct in my body is telling me to just – run. Not because he was going to do anything to me but just –

CLARE. Yeah.

FRANCIS. But instead I – and maybe it's because I had just spent the previous hour thinking about gratitude, or maybe it was just divine intervention but. Instead of running away I started walking towards him. And he startled when he saw me – he was probably surprised to see another person. So he freezes. And I walked up to him, my heart pounding. And as I get closer, I just. I see his face. Two collapsed holes where a nose should be. Sunken eyeholes. Skin just eaten away. Literally like. Worse than I could have expected. It's just. Gross. But instead of revulsion I just felt. Pity. This poor fucking creature. So I walked up to him, and I kissed him on the lips.

CLARE.... what?

FRANCIS. I gave him a kiss.

CLARE.... on the lips?

FRANCIS. On his peeling, leprous lips.

CLARE.... why??

FRANCIS. Because I felt so overwhelmingly sorry for him. And it was a way for me to show affection to someone who has been cast away by literally all of society.

CLARE.... Was he weirded out?

FRANCIS. No!

Then:

I mean he was definitely surprised. I also gave him all the money I was carrying. The point of this is that – sorry if I'm talking too much, you just came to me for advice so –

CLARE. No, please!

FRANCIS. My point is just. Now if I hear a leper bell my chest doesn't seize up. I don't get the anxiety about like. Oh god, do I just avoid, do I pretend I don't have any lira. I can look them in the eye now. I can talk, I can help. It's not guilty avoidance anymore.

CLARE. So what you're saying is I need to just muster up my courage, go to the Ponte Vecchio, find a family in need and just, kiss them on the lips.

FRANCIS. I'm saying go deliver your clothes yourself, and if you end up kissing anyone I'll be seriously impressed.

CLARE *stands*.

CLARE. I'm going to.

FRANCIS. Great.

CLARE. 'Cause that is how down with the poor I am. I'm
gonna come back and you won't even recognize me I'm
gonna be so CHILL about poverty.

FRANCIS. You're a paragon of virtue.

CLARE. If you need to find me I'll be under the bridge!!

She backs away, throwing him a stream of kisses.

Scene Eight

*A homeless encampment. Tents are set up next to each other,
with the occasional shopping cart piled high with stuff.
Bright-blue tarps provide shelter from the elements.*

*This should all look contemporary. The modern signifiers of
poverty are as recognizable to* CLARE *as they are to us.*

CLARE, *dressed in a warm cape and holding a bundle of
clothes, very timidly approaches the camp.*

She doesn't see anyone.

CLARE (*quietly*). Hello?

*No one answers. She gently puts down the bundle of clothes
and turns to go, coming face to face with a person, in very
distressed but modern clothing.* CLARE *screams.*

Sorry! Sorry. I startle easily.

THE POOR. You looking for someone?

CLARE. No. No, I wasn't.

THE POOR. What are you doing here?

CLARE. No, I just. I'm going.

CLARE *starts to walk away.*

THE POOR. Hey! Hey!

CLARE. Sorry, me?

THE POOR picks up the bundle of clothes she'd left.

THE POOR. Your bag.

CLARE. Oh. That's actually. I meant to leave it. It's clothes.

THE POOR looks down into the bag.

Yeah, I thought – I was just thinking of the people who live here. And I wasn't sure if you guys needed any clothes so. I brought some.

THE POOR. Oh.

CLARE. Just in case you did need or want them. Here, look.

She takes the bundle, opens it, and pulls out an emerald-green dress.

Okay, well, this – this is my sister's confirmation dress, actually. It's really pretty – I dunno, maybe it's not useful, or maybe you don't –

She gives the green dress to THE POOR.

Just, hold on to it for now, you can decide – oh! Here's a doublet. It looks really warm. I think there are actually matching pants –

She rifles through the bundle.

…hmmm. I really thought.

She rifles.

I really thought there were matching pants. Okay. No matching pants but I think a lot of pants could go with this color. It's maybe a little small for you. So maybe that should be for someone else. But, for you, let's see – hold this.

She reaches back into the bundle and pulls out some shoes. The sole of the left shoe is coming apart.

What size shoe are you?

THE POOR. Nine.

CLARE. See if these will fit. I think they might!

THE POOR *does so*.

I think that looks like it will fit!

THE POOR. No.

CLARE. No. That's too bad. I should probably. I should probably take these home and have them mended. Do you think you'll be able to find other people who can use these things?

THE POOR. Uh. I dunno. Probably.

CLARE. But I wanted to find something for you! You're a tough size.

THE POOR. Do you have a cloak?

CLARE. No...

THE POOR. Oh.

CLARE. Fuck. I don't.

THE POOR. I need a cloak.

CLARE. I'm really sorry – what's your name?

THE POOR. Bianchi.

CLARE. I'm Clare. I'm really sorry. But maybe if you tell me some of the things you need, I can come back. I can get those things and come back.

THE POOR. Okay.

CLARE. Just. Tell me some of the things you need.

THE POOR. Okay. Well. A cloak.

CLARE. Definitely getting cloaks.

THE POOR. Blankets, always.

CLARE. I can get blankets!

THE POOR. Actually like. Any sort of gourds.

CLARE. Gourds?

THE POOR. Yeah for collecting rainwater. For drinking.

CLARE. Easy. What else.

THE POOR. Bandages are always good. Multipurpose. We can use them for wounds and we can use them for shoes. Food. Milk. Straw to sleep on. Candles. Or beeswax for candles. Doesn't need to be beeswax, we can use tallow. Should I stop?

CLARE. No, please keep going.

THE POOR. We could use any sort of tools you have. And maybe anything to keep the tent clean – brooms. Fire strikers. Oh, and wood – it's okay if it's damp. Any sort of wood for fires.We don't have much to burn. Spindles. Ointments. Pans. We can't cook much here but we can cook some. Dry stuffs, dry foods. The bishop brought us a salami for Easter last year. That was nice, we ate that. Some people are sick, and they need to be warm. So anything to keep them warm. And things in small sizes, for children. Linens. It would be nice to use clean linens. Barrels. Oh, and – for the girls. Bodkins. And hair ties.

CLARE *nods. Then, takes off her cloak.*

What are you doing?

CLARE. Take it.

She hands over the cloak. THE POOR *hesitates.*

Take it, please. Please. You're doing me a favor if you take it. I'll be warm, soon, anyway.

THE POOR *takes it. Puts it on.*

THE POOR. This is a really nice cloak.

CLARE. Good.

End of Act One.

ACT TWO

Scene Nine

CLARE, BEATRICE, ORTOLANA *and the servants,* ALMA *and* PEPPA, *are unpacking the gifts that have just arrived from* CLARE*'s suitor.*

It's like Christmas morning, except the presents have come in trunks/are being presented by servants, and all the gifts are for CLARE.

ORTOLANA (*pulling out some bolts of silk*). Look! Clare! Look at these. Aren't these gorgeous colors? We'll get two dresses out of these, these are fantastic.

BEATRICE. Lemme see, hold it up. Oh, wow. I love that.

ORTOLANA. Aren't they beautiful?

BEATRICE. I seriously love that.

CLARE. Pretty.

ORTOLANA (*holding the bolts up for* ALMA *and* PEPPA). See?

PEPPA. Gorgeous!

ALMA. I love the colors.

ORTOLANA. Your boyfriend's got good taste.

   BEATRICE *has meanwhile pulled out a huge rolled-up piece of thick carpet.*

BEATRICE. Ohhhhh. I think I know what this is? Wait, someone help me unfurl – this is actually –

ORTOLANA. Careful with it.

ALMA. Here, let me help…

BEATRICE. Careful it's really –

ALMA. Oh, wow.

BEATRICE. It's really heavy!

ALMA. It's really heavy.

ORTOLANA (*to* CLARE). We'll display all the gifts in the Great Hall for a few weeks, okay?

CLARE. Do we have to?

BEATRICE (*holding the rolled-up tapestry*). Okay, what's the best way to do this?

ORTOLANA. Just so the neighbors can stop by and see what he sent you.

ALMA. I think – you just stay put and I'll walk that way with mine and kinda… unfurl as I go.

BEATRICE. Okay.

   BEATRICE *holds one end of the tapestry while* ALMA *walks, slowly unfurling*.

CLARE. I don't want the neighbors to stop by.

ORTOLANA. That's not very neighborly!

CLARE. It just feels like. Braggy, I don't know.

ORTOLANA. What are you talking about? That's half the fun. People just wanna see what you got.

BEATRICE. Ta-dah!

ALMA. Look!

ORTOLANA. WOW.

BEATRICE. It's a tapestry!!

CLARE. A merry hunting scene. Cool.

ORTOLANA. Where is this gonna go?

ALMA. Did he *commission* this for you?

ORTOLANA. No.

CLARE. I've only known him three months!

ORTOLANA. He must have already had it.

BEATRICE. I like it. I like the dogs.

CLARE. Are those dogs?

ALMA. I thought it was deer.

ORTOLANA. Dogs, I think.

BEATRICE. It's dogs! They're on a leash!

ALMA. Those dogs really look like deer.

PEPPA. Here's another one…

She hands CLARE *a package wrapped in silk cloth.* CLARE
unwraps it to reveal…

CLARE. A book!!

ORTOLANA. Oh, Clare.

BEATRICE. Oh my god! Clare! You've always wanted a book!

CLARE. Wow wow wow wow.

ALMA. Can you read it?

CLARE. Let's see…

She turns to a page, peers at it for a second.

…yes! I can. It's so beautiful.

ORTOLANA. Look at those colors.

CLARE. I know.

ORTOLANA. So vivid.

CLARE. I know.

PEPPA. What should I do with these?

They turn to see PEPPA *holding, like, four cages of live
quail.*

ORTOLANA. What are those?

PEPPA. Quail, I think? There are twelve, in total.

BEATRICE. What??

CLARE. Oh my god.

ORTOLANA (*laughing*). Oh my god!

BEATRICE. This is insane!

ORTOLANA. Did you tell him you liked quail?

CLARE. Maybe? I can't remember.

PEPPA. He listened!

CLARE. Maybe I said something, like, while making polite conversation?

ORTOLANA. I guess they should go in the Great Hall too, what do you think? It's sort of too funny to not share.

BEATRICE. What do you give the girl who has everything? Twelve quail.

ORTOLANA. Will they be alright in there?

PEPPA. Oh, sure, we'll have the boys look after 'em.

ALMA. Are any of them mates, I wonder?

BEATRICE. Oh my god, what if they multiply?

CLARE. I actually really don't like quail that much. Like, I *like* quail, but I'm not like. Constantly craving quail. I'm not quail-obsessed.

BEATRICE. Says the girl with twelve quail.

ORTOLANA. I think it's all very romantic. He's really spoiling you!

PEPPA. Clare can't be spoilt.

ORTOLANA. Well, that's true.

PEPPA. Deserves every last thing.

BEATRICE. And she's gonna give him like, a dozen babies so it'll all even out.

ORTOLANA. Knock on wood.

PEPPA. The Lord willing.

BEATRICE *laughs*.

ALMA (*bringing over a small case*). There's still this one!

ORTOLANA. Are there air holes? Do we think it's something alive?

PEPPA. Beautiful case.

ORTOLANA. Go ahead, Clare.

CLARE *reluctantly takes the case. Opens it. Pulls out a necklace – a good, old-fashioned jewel adorned with pearls and rubies. The* WOMEN *gasp. Their voices all instinctively fall to the reverent whisper of being in the presence of a really extravagant gift.*

(*Whispered.*) Oh, Clare.

BEATRICE. Oh my god, are you kidding me?

PEPPA. Wow. That is –

BEATRICE. Get outta here with that. That is so gorgeous.

ALMA. Stunning.

ORTOLANA. It is exquisite.

BEATRICE. That is the most gorgeous necklace I have ever seen.

ORTOLANA. Oh my god, it's rubies, it looks like?

PEPPA. And pearls.

BEATRICE. Clare, that is a fucking *jewel*. That is so pretty.

ORTOLANA. I know this goes without saying but you must write to him immediately.

ALMA. It's the most beautiful thing I've ever seen.

CLARE. Here. You take it.

She holds the jewel out to ALMA.

ORTOLANA (*laugh*). What?

CLARE. I mean it! You can have it.

ORTOLANA. She's joking.

CLARE. I'm not joking. Take it!

PEPPA. *Don't* take it –

ALMA. I'm not!

CLARE. No, I'm giving it to her! I don't want it.

ORTOLANA. What do you mean?

PEPPA. Don't you like it, sweetheart?

CLARE. No. Not as much as she does.

ALMA. No, I was just commenting!!

ORTOLANA. You don't have to wear it.

CLARE. I'm not going to wear it.

PEPPA. Well, she'll have to wear it when he comes to visit.

ORTOLANA. That's true, you should wear it then – but other than that – we can keep it somewhere for you – as an asset –

CLARE. I don't want to keep it, I want to give it to Alma.

ALMA. I don't want it –

ORTOLANA. You can't, I'm sorry, but you can't.

PEPPA (*to* ALMA). You shouldn't have been fawning over it –

ALMA. I wasn't –

PEPPA. Now she feels pressure to give it to you –

CLARE. I don't feel pressure, I just *want* to!

BEATRICE. Give it to me, if you want to give it away, I'll take it.

ORTOLANA. Beatrice, hush.

CLARE. I don't want to give it to you, I want to give it to Alma.

ORTOLANA. You can't!

CLARE. It's mine, and I can do what I like with it. It doesn't make me happy.

(*To* ALMA.) But it would make you happy, wouldn't it? You like it. Please take it. Honestly. It would make me happy to know you had it. You could do whatever you like with it, you could keep it, you could wear it every day, you could sell it. Whatever you want. Take it, please. I'm giving it to you. As a friend.

Everyone turns to ALMA. *She looks around to everyone staring at her.*

ALMA. No thank you, ma'am.

ORTOLANA. There, you see? She doesn't even want it.

PEPPA. What would she even have done with something like that?

BEATRICE. I'll take it.

ORTOLANA. Beatrice.

PEPPA. I think in time, you're going to appreciate it more.

ORTOLANA. That's what I think. You never have to wear it, just keep it as an asset. And you might change your mind one day! You might when you're a little older find you can pull it off! I agree that it's a very heavy look for a young girl.

PEPPA. He's just giving you this because he loves you and wants you to have beautiful things! It's okay to have beautiful things.

ORTOLANA. It's not like you get something like this every day.

PEPPA. No! This is a once-in-a-lifetime gift!

ORTOLANA. Just keep it for a little bit and then when you get married, and there's no fear of insulting him, you can decide. Okay?

CLARE *nods.*

Is that all? Have we opened everything? What's in that one, Beatrice?

BEATRICE *looks in a case.*

BEATRICE. Oooooh! A cup!

Scene Ten

In the piazza, a BEGGAR *crosses back and forth, bowl outstretched.*

BEGGAR. Ladies and gentlemen, I am sorry to bother you, may I please have a moment of your time. I am currently homeless, and I am a veteran. I fought in the war against Gubbio, where unfortunately my horse got killed right from under me. When I returned home to my village, I found that my town had been sacked, and the lord of the manor had abandoned the vassals and left for Savoy. I walked all the way here, sleeping in ditches in the side of the road, relying on alms from passing travellers. I am cold, I am hungry, I just want to work and earn a spot to sleep in, covered away from the elements.

CLARE *enters, walks directly over to him.*

I am actively seeking employment as a laborer or land-tiller. I would love to get something to eat, or any spare change you have. No amount is too small.

She drops the ruby necklace into his cup.

CLARE. Be well.

Scene Eleven

Back at the little church. FRANCIS *and* CLARE *chat as they work.*

FRANCIS. So like, a live donkey, a horse, a cow.

CLARE. Were there cows?

FRANCIS. I think there was an ox.

CLARE. Oh, uh-huh.

FRANCIS. There's an ox at the farm down the road.

CLARE. Sheep.

FRANCIS. Obviously sheep.

CLARE. There were probably chickens?

FRANCIS. Meh.

CLARE. You don't think there were chickens?

FRANCIS. I mean, probably but I doubt the chickens played a huge part. I doubt the chickens were cradling the baby.

CLARE. I don't know.

FRANCIS. If there were chickens they were just like. Probably pretty unaware of the goings-on.

CLARE. Maybe they were lovingly cooing.

FRANCIS. No. They weren't lovingly cooing.

CLARE. Okay. It was just a suggestion!

FRANCIS. I'm not going for historical accuracy, it's more about an ambiance.

CLARE. I feel bad for the bishop.

FRANCIS. What do you mean?

CLARE. Well, first you become like, pen pals with the pope.

FRANCIS (*pleased*). Yeah.

CLARE. And just when he's about recovered from that he's gonna hear that you're bringing livestock into the aisles so they can celebrate Christmas with us.

FRANCIS. It's a recreation!

CLARE. Some could say it's idolatry.

FRANCIS. It's one thing to think about the baby in the manger and the angels and 'no room at the inn'. It's going to be another to SEE a baby, an actual baby, in a stack of straw, his frightened parents, no fire, no blankets. I mean I want people to really *get* what it was like, that this family was *poor* and desperate. I don't think anyone understands that anymore.

CLARE. Who is going to give you their *baby*?

FRANCIS. Someone will. People love me.

CLARE. Okay well you've got an ox and a baby. You still need Mary, Joseph, the shepherds, the wise men, and the angels.

FRANCIS. I've got an angel, don't I? You're the angel. I mean, obviously. You look different, by the way.

CLARE. It's 'cause I'm wearing a hairshirt under this, so my clothes are probably fitting a little differently. The bodice isn't as snug as it –

FRANCIS. Actually I think it's your hair.

CLARE. Oh!

Her hand flies up to her head, and she feels around.

Oh. Does it look bad?

FRANCIS. Just different.

CLARE. I've been doing it myself.

FRANCIS. Why?

CLARE. Just. I dunno. I felt a little weird about my lady's maids just constantly…

FRANCIS. Serving you…

CLARE. Waiting on me, I guess, yeah.

They work in silence for a bit.

FRANCIS. I guess I won't be seeing you around that much.

CLARE. You will! I mean. Not when we're at the summer house, I guess, but other than that.

FRANCIS. Summer house.

CLARE. I know. Shut up. I know.

FRANCIS. It's okay, I'm just –

CLARE. But I know –

FRANCIS. I'm not –

CLARE. Yeah, but just. I know. I know how it sounds.

FRANCIS. I'm just curious as to whether you'll be getting an autumn and a spring house in addition to –

FRANCIS *takes off his hood to wipe his brow to reveal his newly tonsured head. (You know, like a friar.)* CLARE *screams.*

Whoa, whoa, what??

CLARE. No!

FRANCIS. *What?*

CLARE. Your hair!

FRANCIS. Oh. Yeah.

CLARE. Why? Why did you do that?

FRANCIS. It's tonsured.

CLARE. Is that a thing?

FRANCIS. Yeah, it's a thing.

CLARE *stares at it.*

CLARE. Why is it like – a circle –

FRANCIS. It's a crown.

CLARE. Of hair?

FRANCIS. Yeah.

CLARE. Why??

FRANCIS. I dunno. St Peter wore his hair like this? It signals a commitment to God?

CLARE. The bishop doesn't have hair like that.

FRANCIS. Well! That tells you something about the bishop's commitment to God.

CLARE. Or his dignity.

FRANCIS. Come on. Does it look that bad?

CLARE *gives a weak shrug.*

Well, whatever. I'm renouncing vanity. We should all spend less time caring about what we look like. I mean, you are!

CLARE. I still care! I'm just bad at braiding.

FRANCIS. Well, whatever.

CLARE. You're really not pivoting into a more moderate approach.

FRANCIS. Nope.

CLARE. Well. Good for you.

FRANCIS. You should join me.

CLARE. *Join* you?

FRANCIS. I mean – yeah.

CLARE. What would that even mean? What would I do?

FRANCIS. What I do. Serve the poor. Work hard. Live humbly.

CLARE. Live *where*?

FRANCIS. Here?

CLARE. Can you imagine?

FRANCIS. I'm being serious actually. That could actually be really great. It's one thing for me to do this. But if *you* do it – I mean if *you* decided to live this lifestyle –

CLARE. But I'm getting married next month.

FRANCIS. Then I guess you'll be waited on, living ostentatiously, and working not at all!

CLARE. You know, I'm not like, the worst. I think I'm a good person!

FRANCIS. Okay!

CLARE. And I'm still going to like. Do charity, probably even more than I do now.

FRANCIS. I'm sure you will.

CLARE. Not everyone can just give up their whole life! I have to believe that there's a way to have a semblance of a normal existence and still, like, help people, there's a middle ground.

FRANCIS. No, there isn't.

CLARE. Come on!

FRANCIS. There isn't! Because to be rich – not even rich! To have any amount of wealth! Means that you on *some* level are okay with people having less than you do. And if you don't think that's the truth, you're kidding yourself. You have nice clothes because someone made them for less money than what you paid. You eat food because someone else is out there tilling the land, picking the fruit, washing it, cooking it, scrubbing the pots after. If they had as much money as you do, they wouldn't be doing that work. And you wouldn't have nice clothes, you wouldn't have all your banquets, your feasts, your breakfasts. It's a system that works *only* if there are people on the top and people on the bottom. And it *only* works because the people at the top agree that they deserve more than the people on the bottom. I don't know that there's a *better* system. I just know I can't be a part of this one. If you're rich, then you're tacitly okay with inequality. There is no middle ground.

CLARE *takes this in.*

Can I ask you something?

CLARE. Yeah, go ahead.

FRANCIS. Would it look any better if the hairline was maybe like, half a centimeter higher?

CLARE *looks at him. Considers.*

CLARE. No...

FRANCIS. No?

CLARE (*shaking her head*). Mmm-mmm.

Scene Twelve

CLARE *is dressed for bed, wearing a brown scratchy-looking nightshirt.*

BEATRICE, *also dressed for bed, but in a muslin nightgown, enters. She stops short when she sees CLARE.*

BEATRICE. No.

CLARE. What?

BEATRICE. I'm not sleeping with you if you're wearing that.

CLARE. Don't be dramatic.

BEATRICE. I hate that thing. I think it has fleas.

CLARE. It doesn't have fleas.

BEATRICE. Then what are all these red spots on my arm? And on my leg?

CLARE. Maybe you have fleas?

BEATRICE. It gives me hives every time I rub against it, look!

CLARE. Well stop rubbing against it.

BEATRICE. IT'S A SMALL BED.

CLARE. Okay, I'll try to stay on my side tonight.

BEATRICE. No! I'm serious. I really hate that thing.

CLARE. Beatrice –

BEATRICE. Look, you have literal welts from it!

She walks over and pulls down the shirt. It's true. CLARE *does have welts.*

Oh my god! Look at this!

CLARE. Where? Barely!

BEATRICE. You look creepy in it, really creepy.

CLARE. Oh my god who cares what I look like. It's to sleep.

BEATRICE. But I. Can't. Sleep. When. You're. Wearing. That.

CLARE. You lead a very pampered life, my darling.

BEATRICE. What does that mean?

CLARE. It means if having a limb occasionally chafe against my shirt at night is the worst of your problems, then I think you can really count yourself blessed.

BEATRICE. Oh, am I? Am I really blessed, Clare? Good to know, 'cause I had fallen into doubt in the *ten minutes of the day when you failed to remind me of it*.

CLARE. Why does it bother you so much? I feel like this is really about you.

BEATRICE. Take the fucking shirt off, Clare.

CLARE. Calm *down*.

BEATRICE. I. AM. Calm!

CLARE *laughs*.

CLARE. Oh my god, listen to yourself.

BEATRICE. NO. Stop making me the crazy one! I am not the crazy one! *I* am not the crazy one.

BEATRICE *screams in frustration, and leaves the room.*

CLARE *lets out a little laugh.*

BEATRICE *enters again. New tact. Very calm.*

Okay, hi.

CLARE. Hi…

BEATRICE. I just got frustrated because I don't feel like you're hearing me out. And I would like you to hear me out.

CLARE. Okay.

BEATRICE. I really respect your decision to wear the hairshirt under your clothes during the day. I support you in that. I admire the strength of your convictions. It's cool that you want to be reminded of suffering at literally any given moment. If that's what you have to do to make yourself feel better – fine. But I'm not sleeping next to that shirt. I'm sorry, but I mean it. It weirds me out and causes me physical discomfort.

CLARE. Fine.

BEATRICE. *Thank* you.

CLARE. I'll sleep on the floor.

BEATRICE.…what??

CLARE. You don't want to sleep with the hairshirt. So I'll sleep on the floor! Everyone's happy!

BEATRICE. You can't sleep on the floor.

CLARE. Why not?

BEATRICE. Because you aren't a dog?

CLARE. Don't be such a princess.

BEATRICE. What about the cold?

CLARE. I'll throw down a blanket.

BEATRICE. What about *the rats*?

At this, CLARE *falters for a second – but just a second.*

CLARE. That's okay.

BEATRICE. That's *okay*??

CLARE. Lots of people sleep on the floor, Beatrice!! I'm doing something that thousands of people do every single day.

BEATRICE. Thousands of people do not sleep on the floor next to a perfectly good bed, that is not something thousands of people are doing every night!

CLARE. Alma and Peppa probably sleep on a floor.

BEATRICE.… yeah! Next to a FIRE! With like twelve other people, not weird and alone in a BEDroom next to a bed.

CLARE. A floor's a floor. Anyway this won't be your problem for much longer.

BEATRICE. Please, Clare. I cannot keep my eyes open, I just want to go to bed.

CLARE. Great. Let's go to bed.

BEATRICE. Where are you gonna –

CLARE. On the floor.

BEATRICE. Jesus.

CLARE *gets on the floor. Gets settled.*

CLARE. It's really not bad –

BEATRICE. You look *so* pitiful right now.

CLARE *cracks a smile.*

Seriously. I could cry.

The two look at each other and crack up.

CLARE. It's so bad. My back like – ow.

BEATRICE. Here, take this pillow at least.

She throws down the pillow, which hits CLARE *in the face.*

CLARE (*laughing*). Ow!

BEATRICE *leans down from the bed and lightly tickles* CLARE*'s feet.*

BEATRICE. Oh my god, a huge rat!!

CLARE *SHRIEKS and pulls her knees up to her chest.*

CLARE. That's not even funny. That's not even funny.

BEATRICE. You. SCREAMED!!!

CLARE. That's not even funny. Oh my god.

BEATRICE. See you in the morning unless you've been eaten.

BEATRICE *settles down into bed and closes her eyes.* CLARE *rolls on her side. After a moment –* CLARE *YELPS.*

What?!?!

CLARE*'s laughing again.*

CLARE. I thought I felt something!!

BEATRICE. Oh my god.

CLARE. Sorry.

BEATRICE. Oh my god.

They laugh.

Scene Thirteen

CLARE *tries on her wedding dress.*

CLARE *is wearing a beautiful, ornate dress. It's the most sumptuous thing we've seen her in so far, but she looks upset, her arms are crossed.*

ORTOLANA, PEPPA *and* ALMA *are all standing around her, in various states of agitation.*

ORTOLANA. *You* chose this. You chose the fabric you chose the color you chose the cut.

CLARE. I know.

PEPPA. I made it wrong. I messed something up.

CLARE. No.

ORTOLANA. No, you didn't.

PEPPA. I tried to make the stitching as tiny as I could but I will say, my eyesight is not what it was –

CLARE. The stitching isn't the problem. It's the dress.

ORTOLANA. I think you look beautiful. Really really elegant and beautiful.

CLARE. It's tacky.

ORTOLANA. What are you *talking* about? It's not tacky.

CLARE. I think it is.

ORTOLANA. We made this to *your* specifications!

CLARE. I know. It's my mistake, my bad taste.

ORTOLANA (*to* PEPPA *and* ALMA). What do you guys think?

PEPPA. Very classy. Very elegant.

ALMA. I think it's so pretty.

ORTOLANA. Not tacky?

PEPPA. Not tacky.

ALMA. Definitely not tacky.

ORTOLANA. See?? Everyone really likes it! No one thinks it's tacky!

CLARE. Okay. Fine. Great.

ORTOLANA (*to* PEPPA *and* ALMA). Can you give us a minute?

PEPPA *and* ALMA *nod and quickly exit.*

I want you to be happy.

CLARE. I know.

ORTOLANA. So please just. Help me figure out how to make you happy.

CLARE. I want something simpler.

ORTOLANA. I personally don't think this is a very ornate dress –

CLARE. The sleeves?? The beading??

ORTOLANA. Okay.

CLARE. It's just. It's not *me*, it doesn't feel like me.

ORTOLANA. Okay, what feels like you?

CLARE. Simpler.

ORTOLANA. Okay.

CLARE. Just like. You know. A tunic.

ORTOLANA. A tunic??

CLARE. God –

ORTOLANA. I was just clarifying! You want a tunic. Okay! Your day.

CLARE. Just nothing showy.

ORTOLANA. Simple. I get it!

CLARE. I was also thinking. It would be nice to like. Feed the poor. In honor of the day.

ORTOLANA. Okay. That's lovely. We can definitely do that.

CLARE. Like maybe we could just skip the big meal and donate all the food.

ORTOLANA. Okay… I like that in principle, I do, my only worry is, if we donate our meal then what will our guests eat?

CLARE. I mean I don't think I'll be very hungry and I don't want to like. Feast.

ORTOLANA. Define 'feast'.

CLARE. Like, ridiculous amounts of food that no one eats and then just gets thrown away. And it's so much wasted food.

ORTOLANA. I can make sure that all the uneaten food gets donated. That's a *lovely* gesture. See?? This doesn't have to be anything you aren't happy with. What else?

CLARE. I'd like to give my dowry to the poor. At least some.

ORTOLANA. I'll talk to your uncle. We can get everything figured out.

CLARE. Okay.

ORTOLANA. Clare.

CLARE. What.

ORTOLANA. Can we do a thought experiment?

CLARE. No.

ORTOLANA. Just humor me.

CLARE. Fine…

ORTOLANA. Just. Imagine a world in which everyone is happy and everyone has had every opportunity that you have. Which isn't true of course because as we know the world isn't like that. But just for a second imagine it. No poverty, no inequality.

CLARE. Yeah, I get it, I'm imagining.

ORTOLANA. If you didn't have to worry about everyone else, and you didn't feel so guilty… would you be happy with this dress?

CLARE *looks down at the dress. The way it skims her waist. The neckline. The richness of the fabric.*

CLARE (*in a small voice*). Yeah. Maybe. I guess.

ORTOLANA. You know I actually understand what you're feeling right now. You think I don't, but I actually do.

CLARE *raises her eyebrows, disbelieving.*

The first time I went to the Holy Land…

CLARE. Mom –

ORTOLANA. No, listen. Little kids followed us everywhere. *Little* kids. All bones and huge eyes, hands outstretched. We gave them everything we had. Things that were meant as gifts, provisions, I mean literally the bread out of our mouths. Not just me, the servants, the translators, everyone, we gave all our food, sometimes our clothes. And it wasn't enough. For every child you fed there were twelve more. And we knew that if the children weren't eating, then the parents were even worse off. Because any parent will make sure his child eats before he does. It was misery. And then on the way home, we stopped in Venice. And suddenly everywhere I looked there was so much food. And seeing all that excess, my first day back on home land, and thinking of all the people who have so little of it – I just. I threw up. Into a canal. In public.

CLARE. Oh my god.

ORTOLANA. I mean how do you just go back to normal life after seeing something like that? It still really upsets me when I think about it. It still makes me sick.

CLARE. That's how I feel.

ORTOLANA. I know. You feel like your life has been very very sheltered and very very naive.

CLARE. And empty.

ORTOLANA. And everything loses its appeal. And you think you might *actually* go to Hell. Like you're the *bad* guy.

CLARE. That's how I feel. But I don't want to feel differently because that would mean deciding to not care, do you know what I mean?

ORTOLANA. Yes. So then you just, walk around feeling terrible and helpless all the time.

CLARE. So what do I do? What should I do?

ORTOLANA. I'll tell you what I did. I had you.

CLARE. What?

ORTOLANA. I had children. I had you. And it's not that it made me forget the suffering that exists – but it did reshuffle things a bit. Because all of the sudden I had you to take care of, to worry about. And all I cared about is your happiness, your well-being. Clare, you're never going to help everyone out there who needs help. But you are going to do everything you can for your kids and that will give you a sense of purpose and contentment that you can't even imagine. I *promise*.

She turns back to CLARE's *dress, her gown, her appearance.*

Now. What are you thinking in terms of hair? Maybe a coronet? Or maybe just loose. Simple, like you said. All those locks just streaming down the back in pretty waves. I think that would be nice. You're going to look so. Beautiful.

Scene Fourteen

Night-time in the little run-down church. Some candles have been lit and placed here and there among the scaffolding.

CLARE *is sitting on the steps of the altar, her head in her hands.*

FRANCIS *enters, with some bread and a bowl of water.*

FRANCIS. You hungry?

CLARE *shakes her head, no.*

Well I brought you some bread.

CLARE. Thanks.

FRANCIS. You just have to dip it in water, otherwise it's kinda hard.

He places the bread and bowl next to her.

You okay?

She nods.

You kinda seem like you're freaking out –

CLARE. I'm okay.

FRANCIS. Do you think anyone saw you leave?

CLARE. I don't think so. I went through the death door. No one guards it.

FRANCIS. And then?

CLARE. No, no one was out.

FRANCIS. Good. That's great.

CLARE. They won't realize I'm gone until morning, and they won't come looking until, I don't know. After lunch.

FRANCIS. Wait, who will come looking?

CLARE. My uncle? His men?

FRANCIS. Oh.

You think he'll do that?

CLARE. I mean, yeah.

FRANCIS. I thought your family would just like – disown you.

CLARE. Well, yeah, but they'll probably try to get me back first.

FRANCIS. Okay.

I didn't really realize.

CLARE. For all they know you kidnapped me.

FRANCIS. I didn't –

CLARE. I know, and I'll tell them that.

FRANCIS. I was gonna move you tomorrow but now I'm wondering if I should do it sooner.

CLARE. Move me? Where?

FRANCIS. San Damiano, it's this other old church I found.

CLARE. Who's there?

FRANCIS. No one. It's perfect.

CLARE. I'm not staying here with you?

FRANCIS. Well no – you're gonna be cloistered. That means –

CLARE. I know what cloistered means I just.

So I'm going to be all alone?

FRANCIS. Well, the goal of course is for more women to join you down the line.

He holds up a brown tunic.

When you're ready, you can change into this.

CLARE. It looks exactly like yours.

FRANCIS. Yeah.

CLARE. Oh.

I guess I thought I would have kind of a… dress.

FRANCIS. No, it's a robe.

CLARE. Yeah, no –

FRANCIS. If you wanted to have it made into a dress you can, I just didn't really know –

CLARE. Sure –

FRANCIS. Like, how to do that. And a robe is basically a dress.

CLARE. Yep.

FRANCIS. It's not the best in cold temperatures, 'cause, you can see, it's kind of porous…

CLARE. Oh. Yeah.

FRANCIS. So what I do is just layer blankets on when I go outside, kinda just wrap myself up in them. Like a shawl. Usually two will do the trick, unless it's *really* freezing. But with blankets it's actually pretty nice and cozy.

CLARE. Okay.

FRANCIS *hands her the robe, then turns around to face the wall.*

Oh, now.

Gingerly, CLARE *starts to undress, with some difficulty unlacing the stays. She slips it off. Then steps into the brown tunic. She very, very gently and carefully folds her dress.*

Okay.

FRANCIS *turns around.*

FRANCIS. Great. Did you wear shoes here?

CLARE.… Yeah, I wore shoes here.

FRANCIS. Okay. You'll probably want to get rid of those or donate them or something. What are they, cowhide?

CLARE. Deerskin.

FRANCIS. Oh wow, deerskin. Okay, so yeah, I would probably renounce those.

CLARE. Okay.

Like, now, or…?

FRANCIS. Yeah, why don't you go ahead and hand them to me now.

CLARE *nods, and slips off her shoes.*

I also just really like deer so it's sad for me to think of them like. Turned into shoes.

She hands her shoes to FRANCIS.

Great. Thanks. We'll put these in the 'donate' pile. Make sure to watch for nails in here, I think I've been pretty good about picking them up but just in case I missed one. Otherwise it's nice and smooth in here. Right outside is fine, too, I would just avoid the chicken coop. But it's actually amazing how your feet get used to all sorts of terrain. It hurts for like a day, but then this, like, padding? Starts to form?

He reaches down and feels the bottom of his foot.

I don't know if it's like, calluses or what but it's pretty protected, almost like a hide that sort of develops –

CLARE *lets out a sob. He looks at her, startled.*

CLARE (*immediately recovering*). I'm sorry.

She composes herself.

Sorry.

FRANCIS. You don't have to apologize.

CLARE. I'm okay. I'm okay. I don't even know why I'm crying right now.

FRANCIS. Really? It seems pretty understandable.

CLARE. I don't want you to think I'm not happy to be here.

FRANCIS. Oh. That's okay.

CLARE. Did you cry when you left?

FRANCIS. I didn't, no, but that's because my dad's a dick, and your family actually seems pretty nice –

CLARE *lets out another involuntary sob.*

CLARE. Sorry.

FRANCIS. It's okay! It's okay.

CLARE. Sorry. It's really. Uhm.

They sit there, CLARE *scrambling in vain to get a grip on her tears, while* FRANCIS *stares stoically ahead, letting her have some privacy.*

She sniffles, wipes her eyes, to no avail.

FRANCIS. Hey...

Unable to bear it any longer, he puts his arm around her. She sobs into his shoulder.

Hey. Hey. It's okay.

CLARE (*through her tears*). It's just because it's new. You know?

FRANCIS. Yeah.

CLARE. I'm going to be fine. It's just a big change. I've never actually been away from my home before, except for once two years ago when we went to stay with my aunt in Gubbio for Lent and I actually cried the whole time because I was homesick, but then when I came back to Assisi I was like 'That was so fun, when are we going back to Gubbio?' and I *meant* it, which just goes to show that I process things in this weird way where I sometimes get overwhelmed in the moment but ultimately see it totally differently once I'm just a little more clear-headed and have had time to process.

FRANCIS. Okay.

CLARE. It's also like – what time is it?

FRANCIS. Oh, I don't know, I didn't count. Two? Three?

CLARE. Okay, yeah. I always get more emotional when I'm tired. And at night. Everything's worse at night. Is what my mom always says…

Her voice shakes.

Honestly I'm probably just going to keep crying until I go to sleep, at this point. It's just like. Once it starts.

FRANCIS.…maybe this…

CLARE. What?

FRANCIS. I dunno.

…maybe this wasn't the best idea.

She looks at him, wide-eyed.

CLARE. No! It was a good idea.

FRANCIS. I dunno…

CLARE. I'm *fine*. I'm just tired but – look! I'm fine! It's not a reflection of… *anything*, it's just emotion!

FRANCIS. Yeah I know, I'm just kind of. Second-guessing. Maybe we haven't really thought this through – Like what are you going to *do*, you can't go door-to-door, are you just gonna stay in all day?

CLARE. I'll be cooking, and cleaning, and mending. I can care for the sick.

FRANCIS. Do you know how to do any of that stuff?

CLARE. I mean it's not hard!

FRANCIS. Maybe it's not fair to take a girl away from her family and house.

CLARE. Not a house! Remember. A palazzo –

FRANCIS. From her home –

CLARE. Lots of girls all over don't have homes, you're not inventing something here.

FRANCIS. But why add to the blight?

CLARE. Because if you're not part of the blight you're causing it??

FRANCIS. Yeah, but. Come on. You're not causing anything.

CLARE. I was complicit in a system that's *built* on the oppression of others...

FRANCIS. I just wonder if I should have maybe run this by the bishop.

CLARE. No! Fuck the bishop!

FRANCIS. I know, I know, but in all honesty, the bishop has been doing this a long time, and he's been pretty chill lately about –

CLARE. No, I'm serious, FUCK the bishop! What are you TALKING about?!

FRANCIS. I just want to think things through. I mean. I dunno! I dunno, I dunno that I'm ready to have like. Disciples!

CLARE. Yes you are. Because disciple number one just fucking snuck out of her house through the goddamn DEATH DOOR ready to pledge her life to you.

FRANCIS. But that's what I'm saying!!! That's what I'm freaking out about right now. You shouldn't be pledging your life to me! I don't want you to get the wrong idea!

CLARE. About what?

FRANCIS. About me and my ultimate dedication to this lifestyle!

    CLARE *gapes at him.*

CLARE. Francis, *what*?!

FRANCIS. I'm just trying to be honest with you, like really fucking honest.

CLARE. You *believe* what you preach...

FRANCIS. Yeah! Of course I do! But also, realistically, it's only been like a year, and before that I was trying to make it as a soldier. And then I found this! And I believe it, I love it, I live it but the prospect of having you totally ruin your life to join me is a lot of responsibility! It just really binds *me* to this in a way I maybe hadn't grappled with before, I dunno –

CLARE. I broke my engagement. I sleep on the floor with rats. I just left my family in the *dead* of night –

FRANCIS. And I don't think you should have done that for me!

CLARE. I DIDN'T do it for you!

FRANCIS. Sorry. Yeah. For God.

CLARE. For what I… believe in!! I'm breaking the cycle. I'm not going to live my life as just another person with enough of a social conscience to feel guilty but not enough conviction to *do* anything different, this is what *you've* taught me!

FRANCIS. I know. I know. I'm just saying… think about it. Clare. Because it's not too late. I could walk you back up the hill, you could sneak back into your room, into your bed, and when everyone wakes up tomorrow morning, no one would be the wiser. And you can like. Be a good person. You can donate to the poor, you can volunteer. And honestly, you might be more useful to people like that. It was helpful having a beautiful young maiden on our side! Just. I don't want you to do something you can't take back.

CLARE *looks at him. Grabs scissors, and hands them to* FRANCIS.

What's this –

CLARE. Take me seriously. Cut off my hair.

She reaches back and quickly starts unbraiding her hair.

FRANCIS. Are you kidding? No.

CLARE. Tonsure me.

FRANCIS. I'm not going to do that.

CLARE. They won't want me back this way. Cut it.

FRANCIS. I can't!

CLARE. Your hair is tonsured.

FRANCIS. I'm a guy.

CLARE. So?

FRANCIS. It would look hideous on you.

CLARE. It looks hideous on you.

She hands him the scissors.

Come on.

FRANCIS. I'm not going to do that. I really don't want to do
that.

CLARE. If I think about the state of the world for like, a *second*.
I mean really think about it. Really let myself feel it, all the
injustice, all the inequality – When I do that, do you think
I can for one second give a fuck about what I look like? And
I don't want to have to force myself to think about it. I want to
never for one moment forget it.

FRANCIS. I'm not a bishop. It's not consecrated.

CLARE. Fuck. The. Bishop.

FRANCIS *hesitates*.

FRANCIS. Ahhhh…

CLARE *takes the scissors and cuts off a chunk of her hair.*

CLARE. See? There.

She cuts another chunk.

There! I'll do it.

FRANCIS. Don't!

CLARE. Too late. I'll keep going. I won't stop. I'll be the crazy woman cutting her own hair. I'm already ruined. But if you do it, I'm consecrated. If you do it, it's a ritual.

He hesitates still. She takes the scissors, and makes to cut off another chunk.

FRANCIS. Okay!! Okay.

He holds out his hand. She gives him the scissors.

Kneel in front of me, I guess.

CLARE *does*.

You're gonna repeat after me. I renounce the world and all its vanities.

CLARE. I renounce the world and all its vanities.

FRANCIS. I vow to God poverty, chastity, and obedience.

CLARE. I vow to God poverty, chastity, and obedience.

FRANCIS. Dear God, I pray on behalf of this woman. Please grant her holy poverty that releases her from enslavement to the world and all its false promises.

He bows her head, and with a sigh, cuts her hair, in rough chops, close to the skull. It falls in great locks to the floor.

Scene Fifteen

In the bedroom, BEATRICE *sits in* CLARE*'s wedding dress, as* PEPPA *and* ALMA *braid and twist her hair into another complicated, gravity-defying hairstyle.*

PEPPA. Can I just say? Poverty is terrible in every circumstance. But. For someone who has had a normal life! It must be so cruel to give it all up. Why would you ever want to give it up?

ALMA. I wouldn't!

PEPPA. No!

ALMA. If I had a palazzo and a lady's maid and could sit around all day, I wouldn't give it up.

PEPPA. I wouldn't give it up. Can you imagine?

ALMA. I just think. There's got to be a better way to help people.

PEPPA. Yes. Exactly.

ALMA. Not like it's possible to completely eradicate inequality –

PEPPA. No, that's unrealistic, but something maybe… *less* unequal.

ALMA. Yes just like – a *slight* redistribution.

PEPPA. Yes! No reason to go whole hog. But if everyone could just – move *up* a level.

ALMA. Well, maybe not everyone –

PEPPA. I guess not, no –

ALMA. Like some people are probably fine where they are.

PEPPA. That's right. So maybe like. The top per cent stays put and everyone else moves up a bit –

ALMA. Like a tiny bit.

PEPPA. Just to be a little more comfortable!

ALMA. And enough so that the poor aren't – poor.

PEPPA. Like if instead of the haves and have-nots it was just, the haves and have-mores –

ALMA. Yes!

PEPPA. Without doing anything *radical* –

ALMA. Yeah, nothing has to be radical just –

PEPPA. Just enough so that things were a *little* bit better... I dunno. Wouldn't that be nice?

ALMA. Bodkin?

BEATRICE *hands her one.*

Scene Sixteen

CLARE, *now in a full habit – the first time we've seen her like this. Shorn head covered.*

She lights a candle. Gets down on her knees. And starts to pray.

CLARE. Lord, make me an instrument of your peace.

Let me bring love where there is hate, unity where there is discord.

Let me bring joy where there is pain, and hope where there is despair.

Make me love, not wish for love.

Let me be satisfied by what I have, and not consumed by what I want.

Let me feel that every meal is a boon, every shelter a gift, and to live at all is to live well. Lord, keep me from complaining about the vain and the insignificant.

Help me to overcome my jealousy, my laziness, and my rancor.

Jealousy, which is ingratitude.

Laziness which is ingratitude.

Rancor which is ingratitude.

Help me instead, to remember the millions dying of famine in Yemen. Help me remember *one* of them.

Help me remember the flaccid, stick-like arms of *one* of them. Help me put her in my mind and etch her there, so she is with me when I say 'carnitas and a little rice' at Chipotle, so she is with me when I order toilet paper on Amazon, so she is with me when I tip my Uber driver and rate him five stars.

Lord, give me strength so I don't retreat to the other end of the subway car, pulling my scarf up to my nose, but rather sally forth and ask, 'Do you need any help?', or better yet, say, 'I can help you. I'm going to help you.'

God, help me remember the thirteen-year-old girl walking up Atlantic Avenue with her belly sticking out and her too-small coat unbuttoned in a blizzard, the farmers and shepherds pouring their milk out onto the highway because they'd rather destroy it than sell it for nothing, the man in rags carefully examining the mascaras at Sephora 'cause it's warm in Sephora and the shelter doesn't open for another five hours. And I think 'Poor guy…', as I slip another serum into my basket, and I think 'It's nice that they're letting him browse!' as if he has any less right to be in a store than I do, and I pledge to donate to a GoFundMe campaign when I get home, and that'll be enough to assuage my guilt, and by the time I go to the checkout and select my free sample (because I have enough Insider Points for a free sample, because I've spent enough at Sephora to accrue lots of free samples), by the time I've selected my free sample (a lip exfoliant), I've forgotten about the man in rags who is now perusing the Jo Malone perfumes, and by the time I head outside into the cold and down into the subway I don't even see the six people I pass, one on the steps of the Ukranian church, one huddled on a mattress in front of a Dunkin' Donuts, one at the entrance of the subway, one asking for a swipe outside the turnstiles, and two on the bench on the platform. I don't even see them, and once I've made it back to my apartment (one on the steps of my own subway station and one I pass digging for water bottles in the trash on the corner of my street), once I've made it back to my apartment I've completely forgotten about my pledge to donate (and to what? And does the money even *go* to the right people? So hard to know), which is just as well, because even the process of donating makes me too aware, and I can't really be aware, I can't really *think* about it, because once you start to think about it how can you possibly go on? Once you start to really think about it then you have to make the choice.

Lord help me. Lord help me. Lord help me be good. Don't put me on this Earth just to be selfish. Just to be shitty. Just to think it's too bad but not *do* anything about it. God, help me be good. Help me be good. Help me be good. Dear Lord, help me be good.

CLARE *looks up and waits for God to help her.*

End of play.

A Nick Hern Book

Poor Clare first published in Great Britain in 2025 as a paperback original by Nick Hern Books Limited, The Glasshouse, 49a Goldhawk Road, London W12 8QP, in association with the Orange Tree Theatre, Richmond

Poor Clare copyright © 2025 Chiara Atik

Chiara Atik has asserted her right to be identified as the author of this work

Front cover: artwork design by Thomas Atkinson-Joy; original photos by Theo Afrika and Roy J Baron

Designed and typeset by Nick Hern Books, London
Printed in Great Britain by Mimeo Ltd, Huntingdon, Cambridgeshire PE29 6XX

A CIP catalogue record for this book is available from the British Library

ISBN 978 1 83904 489 2

CAUTION   Professionals and amateurs are hereby warned that *Poor Clare* is subject to a royalty. It is fully protected under the copyright laws of the United States of America and of all countries covered by the International Copyright Union (including the Dominion of Canada and the rest of the British Commonwealth), the Berne Convention, the Pan-American Copyright Convention and the Universal Copyright Convention as well as all countries with which the United States has reciprocal copyright relations. All rights, including professional/amateur stage rights, motion picture, recitation, lecturing, public reading, radio broadcasting, television, video or sound recording, all other forms of mechanical or electronic reproduction, such as CD-ROM, CD-I, information storage and retrieval systems and photocopying, and the rights of translation into foreign languages, are strictly reserved. Particular emphasis is laid upon the matter of readings, permission for which must be secured from the Author's agent in writing. Inquiries concerning rights should be addressed to: William Morris Endeavor Entertainment, LLC, 11 Madison Avenue, 18th Floor, New York, New York 10010, USA; attn: Derek Zasky

www.nickhernbooks.co.uk/environmental-policy

Nick Hern Books' authorised representative in the EU is
Easy Access System Europe – Mustamäe tee 50, 10621 Tallinn, Estonia
email gpsr.requests@easproject.com